Asia in Mobility

Spatial Practices between the Colonial / Imperial and (post)Cold War Borders

EDITED BY

Institute for East Asian Studies
at SungKongHoe University

Jimoondang
Seoul

Jimoondang
85 Gwanginsa-gil, Paju-si, Gyeonggi-do, 413-756, Korea
82 Donhwamun-ro, Jongno-gu, Seoul, 110-360, Korea
227 Suttons Lane, Edison, NJ 08817, USA
Phone: 82-2-743-3096 E-mail: edit@jimoon.co.kr
82-2-743-3192~3 E-mail: sale@jimoon.co.kr
Fax: 82-2-743-0227, 82-2-742-4657
Homepage: www.jimoon.co.kr

The National Library of Korea Cataloging-in-Publication (CIP)
Asia in Mobility: Spatial Practices between the Colonial/Imperial and (post)Cold War Borders / Edited by Cha Seung-ki, Kwon Heok-tae, Cho Kyung-hee, Lee Jeong-eun, Kim Sung-kyung
Paju: Jimoondang, 2012
ISBN 978-89-6297-145-3 93300 349.1-KDC5 327.5-DDC21 CIP2012002976

Printed in Korea

This book was supported by the National Research Foundation of Korea Grant funded by The Ministry of Education, Science and Technology (KRF-2007-361-AM0005)

Preface

Asia in our discussion represents not a solid but a relative and relational space generated and created by the vectors of mobility. From the mid nineteenth century to the present, globalizing impetus, following the trajectory of imperialism, has forged a dependent concept of Asia (or Orient) as the Other vis-à-vis the West. In the meantime, peoples in Asia have been creating new spaces, social and ethnic relations and *lieux de memoire* while experiencing and practicing otherness of the various boundaries, regimes, places, nation-states and cultures. And these mobility practices of nomad, migration, colonization, border-crossing and deterritorialization have evolved following the vectors of mobility within a constellation of histories of capitalism, war, labor, and colonization. This new conceptualization of Asia, constructed through the transnational flows that transcend the cultural, ideological, national and ethnic boundaries as well as post/Cold War divisions, is now opening up multiple but ambiguous spaces for inter-Asian cultural and political practices.

What is at stake is, then, how transcultural practices of the returning migrants through the axes of mobility—whose historical origin is the imperialistic, (post) Cold War and globalizing drive and regulation, can transform Asia into a more democratic and ethical space of every day lives beyond the regional and national boundaries. From the perspective of experiences, perceptions and spatial practices of the mobile subjects, Asia can be broken down into multiple and relative spaces constantly being re-appropriated by the subjects.

For example, to the North Korean defectors crossing the border between the North Korea and China, South Korea is not an adjacent nation but a faraway destination that can be reached only through a detouring journey via China, Mongolia, Laos and the USA.

This transnational mobile subject includes ethnic minorities, migrants, undocumented sojouner, return migrants and people of the ex-colonies who are supposed to position themselves as the others and thus make Asia a relative place.

To these others being caught somewhere betwixt and between places of Asia—particularly when they are mobilized in a different context from that of cosmopolitan experiences at the metropolis in this globalizing era—Asia represents not a solid and holistic concept but flexible, ambiguous and multiple spaces.

Paying attention to spatial relationality of what is presumably called "Asia," SungKongHoe University Humanities Korea Project that has been organized by Institute for East Asian Studies and sponsored by the Korea Research Foundation attempts to historicize mobility in Asia and thus construe a new imagination of inter-Asianness.

Contents

1

Naeji in *Oeji**, or the Colonized in the Metropole:
The (Non)Ontology of Hole

by CHA Seung-ki
Humanities Korea Professor
Institute for East Asian Studies at SungKongHoe University

1. Yobo** Crossing Hyeonhaetan***

So what's this great work, and where do you find it?

......

Actually, it's easy work. This will be my third time already. You contact companies in *naeji*, and then you go and catch *yobos*...... I'm talking about Joseon coolies, workers. Now, you recruit them mostly in South and North Gyeongsang Province. If not, you have to go to Hamgyeong or Gangwon Provinces, and then to Pyeongan Province. But the easiest is to go to South Gyeongsang Province. Hahaha."

---

* In Imperial Japan before and during World War II, *naeji* (内地, literally "inner lands," pronounced *naichi* in Japanese) referred to the mainland of the empire. The other territories of the empire were called *oeji* (外地, literally "outer lands," pronounced *gaichi* in Japanese). http://en.wikipedia.org/wiki/Mainland_Japan -Tr.

** *Yobo*: A term used by Japanese to refer to Korean(s) in a derogatory manner.

*** Hyeonhaetan (玄海灘), today internationally known as Korea Strait, is a sea passage between Korea and Japan. Passenger ships still operate, as during historical times, between Busan and Shimonoseki -Tr.

He paused for a moment here and then cunningly gave out a hearty laugh.[1]

It is the late 1910s. YI In-hwa, a Korean foreign student in Japan, is crossing Hyeonhaetan on his routine return trip to Joseon and overhears this conversation in the bath house aboard the ship. He is shocked to hear a Japanese manpower contractor speak about selling Korean "workers" to companies in *naeji*. The shock has two effects on him. First, he becomes aware that he and the Korean workers share the same national identity; and second he becomes self-critically aware that he was ignorant about rural conditions in Joseon. "Now and then [he] suffered through incidents that got on his nerves; it annoyed, and even angered, him that he would be interrogated in Shimonoseki or Busan, or in Gyeongseong (present day Seoul -Tr.) on his annual visits home, but he soon forgot about them. There were actually few occasions in which the feelings of hostility or defiance curdled up."[2] But, now, as a *yobo* himself, he was enraged. "By no means could the lives of the tenant farmers be so wretched; he had never heard of them." And now he was criticizing himself for having been in an ivory tower, and for his "vanity and thoughtlessness."[3]

Yi In-hwa, too, was a Korean living in Japan, or *naeji*. However, as a foreign student staying in Japan, he did not meet the other Koreans who must have also been there. Indeed, it was probably this "self-awareness" among Korean intellectuals during the colonial time that later set off numerous enlightenment and solidarity movements,[4] but for now, let us only keep in mind

1 YOM Sang-seop (1987), "Mansejeon (Before *manse*)" in *Yeom Sangseop jeonjip* (The complete works of Yeom Sangseop) 1, Mineumsa, 38-39.

2 Ibid., 36.

3 Ibid., 40.

4 After the March 1st Movement in particular, opportunities for such a meeting became at least available, as Korean population in Japan expanded and various organizations were formed in the name of ethnic and/or class connections. For a study on social movements that brought the former peasant population and the student population —the two axes of Korean community in Japan at the time—in contact with each other, see KIM In-deok (1996), *Sikminji sidae Jaeil Joseonin undong yeongu* (A study of the

that a Korean student and Korean peasants aboard the same ferryboat crossing Hyeonhaetan together do not meet each other; let us also keep in mind that it is aboard a ship crossing Hyeonhaetan that the student identifies himself with the peasants in a bitter awakening of a nationalist sentiment.

YI Inhwa and *yobos* could not meet because their trajectories of crossing Hyeonhaetan were completely different. Except in the special cases where they were looking for a "learned position" in the metropole, most students in Korea went over to Japan to further their studies in expectation of raising their social status in Korea upon their return. However, in the case of farmers from the lower stratum of society, who crossed Hyeonhaetan in order to get away from further sliding in social stratum, unemployment, and the vicious cycle of poverty, their purpose in going to the metropole from the beginning was to improve their lot economically. Moreover, while some people crossed back and forth between Korea and Japan, under various circumstances, for more and more Koreans in Japan, the metropole became "the base camp of living" as series of their family members and relative arrived after them. In short, while the students went to the metropole with the overall plan to return to Korea, for members of the poor peasantry for whom life was "a hell if you leave, and a hell if you remain,"[5] a move to Japan meant some thing

---

movement of the Koreans in Japan during the colonial time), Gukhak Jaryowon; and KIM Gwang-yeol (2009), "Jaeil Haninui minjok haebang undong gwa 3.1 undong ginyeom (National liberation movements waged by Koreans in Japan and their commemoration of the March 1st Movement)" in *Hanguk geunhyeondaesa yeongu* (The study of Korean modern and contemporary history), Vol. 50.

However, in the "labor novels" of the 1920s—written by such writers as SONG Yeong and YUN Gi-jeong, champions of "proletariat literature"—it is difficult to find workers and intellectuals meeting each other. We see such encounters in the works of JANG Hyeok-ju and KIM Sa-ryang that appear after the late 1930s, as these writers examine the issues of Korean identity in the context of the discourse of *naeseon ilche*, or the imperial claim that *naeji* and Joseon are "one entity."

5 KAJIMURA Hideki (1993), "8 · 15izenno Zainichi Chosenjinno rekishi (The History of Zainichi Koreans until 8 · 15)," *Collected Works of Kajimura Hideki*, Vol. 6, Akashishoten, 68.

more comprehensive; the move was part of a wider casting of a net by those whose lives were uprooted and who were looking to establish new bases for living.

Many research works have already been carried out, from various aspects, on the subject of these desperate Koreans crossing over to Japan and their everyday life.[6] The large-scale migration of Korean peasants to Japan and their destitute lives there served as one of the most compelling evidences of the reality of the Japanese control and exploitation in colonial Korea and the ethnic discrimination in the imperial system. Thus, on the one hand, most of these studies are an expose of the Japanese exploitation of the colony and their policies of forced mobilizations; many of them focused on verifying incidents of discriminatory ethnic violence perpetrated against migrant Koreans in Japan. The other major focus of these studies, on the other hand, is the restoration of the history of resistance and struggle carried out by migrant Koreans in Japan. These studies, in part, were also connected to attempts to establish Zainichi Korean[#] subjectivity and a critique of Japanese society, where Zainichi Koreans, the largest post-war ethnic group, had long been treated as "invisible people."[7]

In this way, the history of the Koreans who migrated to Japan during the colonial/imperial period has been largely narrated in terms of the relationship between Japan and Korea as the ruler and the ruled, respectively, or in terms of discrimination and

6 Pioneering studies on the formation of Korean communities in Japan during the colonial/imperial period were carried out in the 1950s-60s by such scholars as Kang Jae-eon and PARK Gyeong-sik. For more recent studies, see TONOMURA Masaru (2010), *Jaeil Joseonin sahoeui yeoksahakjeok yeongu* (A historical study of the community of Koreans in Japan), translated by SIN Yu-won and KIM In-deok, Nonhyeong; and KIM Gwang-yeol (2010), *Haninui Ilbon ijusa yeongu: 1910-1940-nyeondae* (A study of the migration history of Koreans migrating to Japan: 1910-1940s), Nonhyeong.

Here and in other parts of this paper, the Korean term "jaeil (在日) Joseonin," or "Korean(s) living in Japan," is translated as "Zainichi Korean(s)" -Tr.

7 TONOMURA Masaru, op. cit., 17.

resistance between the Japanese and Korea. It goes without saying that *naeji* Korean migrant communities were very much the offshoots of the imperial colonization of Korea; thus when dealing with the issues of Korean migration to Japan during this period, it is perhaps natural that the relationship of domination or subordination, or of discrimination and resistance, at the national (*minjokjeok*) level, serves as the central axis around which the research narratives take place. Indeed, without remembering this central axis, the ruler/ruled aspects of class and gender relations will not be understood properly. However, it is also true that the ethnic (*minjokjeok*), class, and gender antagonism between Japan and Korea does not form a perfect symmetry along the national line of empire and colony. These antagonistic relations during the colonial period cross each other, or they are intricately intermixed. For example, Korean manpower contractors and managers at *hamba* (a boarding house usually set up on the premises of a large construction site providing lodging facilities to laborers for a fee) often acted as the intermediary exploiters of Korean workers.

Accordingly, to understand the "site" of *naeji* Korean communities during the colonial/imperial period, the colonial/imperial regime of generating, sealing, and transposing ethnic, class, and gender conflicts must be first set forth as a starting point. Thus, in this paper, I will first examine how Koreans came to settle down in the imperial "home" territory of Japan during the colonial period, and examine the historical site of their community in terms of the day-to-day operation of the colonial/imperial regime. Furthermore, by introducing archival and literary texts that directly relate or symbolically depict the migrant workers' communities and their lives, this paper also examines the (non)ontology of those historical sites.

2. Bodies with Mobility Etched on Them

A colony (植民地) is, first and foremost, a place (地) of transplanting (植) people (民). Accordingly, it could be said that "mobility," whether volunteered or forced, is at the heart of a colonial system. Of course, when people are transplanted, relations are also transplanted. After Hokkaido and Okinawa, Japan carried out the same transplantation experiments in Taiwan and Korea. To grasp the culture, the history, and the land of the colonies, Japanese authorities carried out extensive field surveys of customs (舊慣). However, the process of translating what is the ambiguous Other into something that is graspable through a language that is familiar and statistics was, in itself, already the first stage of transplantation. Furthermore, such transplantation and re-composition of people and relations led to more movements and migrations of the people uprooted within and across the colonial/imperial territories.

In the Japanese colonial/imperial regime, Korea occupied an ambiguous position. It was included as part of the imperial dominion but not as part of *naeji*—as in the cases of Hokkaido and Okinawa, which one could say were also colonies. Thus in terms of rule of law, it was an extra-legal territory vis-a-vis the metropole. It was ruled by laws promulgated by Governor-General of Korea.[8] In other words, Korea was a special zone which was politically controlled by the metropole but where the laws of the metropole did not apply. This fundamentally discriminatory structure inherent in the colonial/imperial regime functioned as the apparatus that set the politics of ethnic exclusion and incorporation in motion. However, the exclusion/inclusion policies were not always consistent, as the policies shifted to adapt to the changing historical exigencies of the Empire. Initially, the colo-

---

8 ASANO Toyomi (2008), *Teikoku Nihonno Shokuminchi Hosei* (The Colonial Legislative System of Imperial Japan), Nagoya University Press; See also YI Seung-il (2008), *Joseon chongdokbu beopje jeongchaek* (The legislative policy of Chosen Government—General), Yeoksa bipyeongsa.

nial/imperial regime championed "integration" while making sure to stamp *naeji/oeji* distinctions on legal and institutional matters. This left room for Korean customs and common laws to continue under the colonial rule. On the other hand, the maintenance of Korean "customs," or what is considered uniquely "Korean," had the effect of identifying pre-modernity as part of Korean national character, which in turn produced an "identity" index, or a basis for denying the colony an equality status with the metropole. This discriminatory structure was turned upside down around the time of the Sino-Japanese War of 1937. In other words, as war mobilization efforts intensified, the arguments for the *naeji* "extension" policy gained strength and the *naeseon ilche* policy was championed; these were attempts to finally integrate *naeji* and *oeji* under the same legal jurisdiction. Finally, around the time of the beginning of the "Greater East Asia War," the imperial government reduces the autonomy of the Governor-General in Joseon and tries to integrate Korea within the jurisdiction of the metropolitan law. On the one hand, this move was designed to include Koreans as Japanese imperial subjects with equal rights and responsibilities as Japanese. On the other hand, it activated violence that attempted to invalidate any indication of ethnic (minjokjeok) differences through the visions of totalitarian assimilation, which included the imperial plans to build a highly militarized state and the rhetoric of the edification of the emperor's less civilized subjects through the "universal benevolence (一視同仁)" of the Emperor. Japan was defeated before these visions of integration became fully realized. However, what is important here is that the *naeji/oeji* differentiation—and the manipulation of that differentiation—was part and parcel of the dynamics on which the colonial/imperial regime was founded and maintained.

At a more fundamental level, it is a well-known fact that the series of modernization "reform" measures taken by colonial authorities in Korea brought about the collapse of the previously existing communal relations, separating the predominant farming population of Korea from the land and producing "free" work force en mass. It is generally understood that, within the context of a single country, this "free" labor force forms the proletariat as the population is absorbed by cities and modern industries in the country and that the surplus labor forces not absorbed in this way form a corps of reserved workforces that float around the peripheries of the working class. However, in the case of colonial Korea, it was impossible for the "freed" labor force to become proletariat; at the beginning of its rule, increasing rice production (*sanmi jeungsik*) was Japan's economic policy for colonial Korea, and modern industries in the country were sparse. Thus the surplus workforce that could not be absorbed within the country moved in various directions; Koreans from the northern part of the country mostly move to Manchuria and present-day Yanbian; those from the central region gravitated toward urban outskirts, or they moved further away from general population and into remote mountain regions to become slash-and-burn farmers; and those in the southern region of the country tended to cross Hyeonhaetan, "the black sea," over to Japan. The migration of Koreans to the metropole, in particular, coincided with the expansion of the reproduction structure of capitalism and increased demand for labor in Japan after the end of the First World War. It was also the period in which increase in state-led public works and civil engineering and construction projects required cheap labor that would withstand dangerous and unsanitary work conditions.[9] There is an additional element that triggered Korean migration to Japan during this time; one cannot ignore the structure of discrimination and gap inherent in the colonial/imperial regime that prompted a collective yearning for civilization, in a

9 See Ken Kawashima (2009), "Sangpumhwa, bulhwakjeongseong, geurigo junggan chakchwi: Jeongangi Ilbonui maknodong sijangeseo ui Joseonin nodongjadeul ui tujaeng (Commodification, Contingency and Intermediary Exploitation: Korean Proletarian Struggles in the Day Labor Market of Interwar Japan)" in Henry EM and GWAK Junhyeok eds., *Geundaeseong ui yeokseol: Hangukhak gwa Ilbonhak ui gyeonggye reul neomeo* (Entangled modernities: Beyond the boundaries of Korean Studies and Japanese Studies), Humanitas.

generic sense, and expectations for improved standards of living among Koreans. In other words, the colonial/imperial regime worked in part by activating a yearning for the metropole, through a "sister from the house next door" who goes to the metropole and comes back smart and stylish.[10]

Given the colonial/imperial regime, the operational foundation of which was carved by the *naeji/oeji* discrimination and gap, what is the meaning of the Korean migration within the region, the imperial sphere, and in particular the Korean migration to the metropole? The migration from Korea to Japan, or from an *oeji* to the *naeji*, meant first and foremost a migration from being a farmer to being a worker, and in particular to a lumpen proletarian. By the time Japan colonized Korea and destroyed Korean peasantry, it was already a country of advanced monopoly capitalism, which meant that the collapse of Korean peasantry occurred when accumulation of capital in Korea was preemptively blocked. Under these circumstances, the uprooting of the farming population from the land and its reorganization into modern society meant population movement within the region of the colonial/imperial sphere. Of course, the population migration from "farmer" to "worker" also took place within Korea, but what is important to note here is that the class segmentation —the rise of the working class out of the farming population—in Korea during this period is linked to the colony-to-metropole migration. That is to say, the colonial/imperial regime produced a massive segment of farming population who were uprooted from—or who became 'economically less dependent' on—land, and the individuals in this population segment had mobility engraved on their body at the level of language, law, and

10 "...those who went to Japan came back pretty, sisters and other people in the neighborhood. If they came here [Osaka], they could have pretty clothes, at least a little bit of them, and I thought I'd like that too (YANG Rye-nyeo, interview with JE Ju-saeng, circa 1912). See SUGIHARA Toru (1998), *Ekkyosuru Tami: Kindai Osakano Chosenjinshi Kenkyu* (Border-crossing People: A Study of Korean's History in Modern Osaka), Shinkansha, 91.

identity.

Furthermore, the class segmentation under the colonial/imperial regime could not take on a normative pattern. The ethnic discrimination against Koreans amplified when Korean peasants migrated to the metropole because of the linguistic and cultural differences. What this meant was that most of Korean migrants in the metropole did not even belong the working class proper but to the class of the lumpen proletariat, whose lives were extremely precarious; they were the reserve force for Japanese industrial labor, and they eked out scanty existence mostly as day laborers. The migration and settlement trajectories of Koreans in Japan show the singular process of dismantling the class system in Korea under the colonial system; they also show the exploitation structure of the colonial/imperial regime that manipulated the labor market by incorporating but at the same time marginalizing the Korean workforce.

3. The Power of Desire Driven by Discrimination

The Koreans in Japan, who mostly lived as lumpen proletarian, gradually began to develop a sense of permanent residency in Japan, even though not much change took place in their largely unstable conditions. A survey result from the mid-1930s shows a high level of a sense of settlement among Koreans in Japan, even if one were to takes into account variables not accounted for in the survey.[11]

It seems that the Koreans in the metropole developed a sense of permanent residency in Japan as their stay became prolonged, and as the base of their everyday lives became the Korean communities that eventually developed in or around neighborhoods

11 See the statistics table on "Permanent Resident Consciousness" of the Koreans living in various cities in Japan. KIM Gwang-yeol, op. cit.; SUGIHARA Toru, op. cit., 208-210.

where the migrants were working. Generally speaking, early migrants form a cluster in or around a certain neighborhood or location. Once they are somewhat established in their new location, serial migration takes place through blood relations and/or regional ties in the homeland. In a typical migration trajectory, a Korean man would leave his farming or fishing village, arrive in a Korean community in Japan; then find work in a local factory or work as a day laborer on a construction site. There are at least two factors to consider in relation to the high level of the sense of permanent residency among Korean migrants in Japan during the colonial/imperial period. First, to the destitute peasantry in general, the cost of crossing Hyeonhaetan and the weight of covering other expenses related to the migration probably posed a significant economic burden.[12] Second, the Japanese policy on Koreans crossing over to Japan fluctuated according to the economic or unemployment condition in the metropole.[13] At least until 1937, when the Sino-Japanese war broke out and Japan began to forcibly mobilizing Koreans en mass, strict regulations and control were in place for the cross-sea migration. Thus, it was not strictly a matter of free will for a Korean migrant to repatriate, or to re-cross the sea to Japan once he came back to Korea. Accordingly, what we find in the backside of the high level of the sense of permanent residency among Korean workers in Japan during this period is, paradoxically, the anxiety of those who whose lives have been uprooted. An article published in *Minjung Sibo* (People's News)[14], a newspaper published by Korean migrants in Korean language, relates the story

12 See KIM Gwang-yeol (2001), Based on statistical data that showed surprisingly large amounts of cash the Koreans crossing over to Japan were carrying and their education level, the author argues that most of the migrants probably came from farming families with above-average means. However, considering that most of the migrants with relatively high amounts of cash were heads of households (p. 32 of the same book), the statistical data show not only the class composition of the Koreans crossing over to Japan but also their strong orientation to settle down in Japan.

13 See KIM In-deok (1996).

14 *Minjung Sibo* (June 15, 1935–September 21, 1936) was a Korean-language newspaper published in Osaka by Marxists and leaders of the migrant Korean community.

of a man by the name of Yi Sin-yeo, who was living in Osaka and was summoned to the police for some reason. For over a month, nobody heard from him. Then, one day his family in Oksaka received a letter from him from Jeju Island, his hometown in Korea. The family found out only then that he was deported to Korea.[15] To the migrant Koreans in Japan at the time "*songhwan* (deportation) .... was the sound of a death knell."[16]

Such anxiety and fear led to some Koreans demanding that Koreans change their traditional beliefs and customs on their own accord:

> If one has any self-respect at all as a worker, one has to perish the thought of loving one's home town or of entertaining homesickness.
>
> Home doesn't have to be where one is born; home is where one works.
>
> There are too many fellows who go back to Korea to accompany a dead body home in Korea for a funeral, who have lost their work and who cannot return to Japan. They are bewildered. The poorer we are, and the harder it becomes to cross the sea at will, we have to liberate ourselves from the ground burial. Otherwise, one dead body can lead to a threat of famine for several living bodies. Let's liberate ourselves from the ground burial. Let us strictly observe cremation.[17]

This article is lamenting those Koreans who cross Hyeonhaetan to give a family member the traditional ground burial in Korea and exhort them to instead practice cremation. It illustrates how the difficulty of re-entering Japan acts to strengthen a commitment to settle down in Japan, and how it can trigger "Japanifi-

---

15 "Gyeongchal e hochul doen gajang han dal hueya songhwani panmyeong! (The deportation of the head of a household becomes known a month after he was summoned to the police!)," *Minjung Sibo*, September 15, 1935.

16 "Joseonin e daehan ganje songhwaneul danyeon pyejihara! Geu pyehaeneun makdaehada!! (Stop the deportation of Koreans! The injuries caused are great!!)," *Minjung Sibo*, September 15, 1935.

17 PS Saeng, "Hwajang eul yeohaeng haja (Let's observe cremation)," *Minjung Sibo*, July 15, 1935.

cation" at the day-to-day level. What is further interesting here is that the argument for abandoning ground burial for cremation is built on the rhetoric of rationality and practicality. Considering the exigencies of the precarious lives, it is rational to replace home with workplace, and ground burial with cremation. However, such rational thinking also has resonance with the imperialist rhetoric of civilization in which the traditional interpretations of life and death are criticized as "formality-bound" and "conventional," and as something that "must be abolished," or as "a superstition believing in the sanctity of a grave."[18]

The Korean migrants in Japan were exposed to ethnic discrimination, class alienation, and lack of legal protection, and there is a strong sense among the Koreans that they must take the lead to rid themselves any irrationalities about them. This obsession often takes the form of self criticism. Some of them feel ashamed of the fact that there is a full array of brokers and gangster groups in the Korean community,[19] and others blame the lack of a sense of public order among Koreans when a Japanese landlord refuse to rent a room to a Korean.[20]

This critical sense based on the rhetoric of "rationality" is directed not only inward but also toward the metropolitan authorities who force discrimination, alienation, and lack of legal protection on Korean migrants. The fact that their demand for fair treatment and their criticism of the authorities' irrationalities are constructed on the rhetoric of "legitimacy" is what is interesting in connection with the site of the Korean migrants in Japan.

... Japan [is] a country that is proud of itself as being a first-rate nation in

18 SUGIHARA Toru, op. cit., 132.

19 Ueundongcheonin [愚隱洞天人], "Daepaneun mubeop cheonji? (Is Osaka a lawless universe?)," *Minjung Sibo*, Inaugural edition, June 15, 1935.

20 Ueundongcheonin, "Jutaeknan munje e daehaya (Regarding the issue of housing shortage)," *Minjung Sibo*, July 15, 1935.

> the world, as being *a country of the rule of law* whose constitution guarantees the separation of the three branches of government, i.e., the legislature, the judiciary, and the executive. And the Great Osaka is the second largest city in such a Japan; it is an industrial city, the economic heart of Japan. But I say to you, here in this splendidly bustling Osaka, it seems in some respect that there is no law and no police.[21]

> Japan is said to be *a country of the rule of law* where its people are governed by the rule of law. Indeed, I would say the Napoleonic Code would pale in comparison. Its legal web is so finely cast, and the police, the court, and the prison system are there to protect and preserve this web. But for us Koreans who live under such rule of law, we wonder time and again, as to whether or not we are in fact living in such a country.[22]

The writer in the article criticizes that in Osaka, the second largest city in a country that is modern and civilized, there are "*lawlessness and policelessness* that would be worse in comparison to a backward village in a remote corner of Joseon which lags far behind Japan in modern civilization."[23] What is interesting about these arguments against the unfair treatment of Koreans in Japan is that they are built on the logic that Japan is a country of the rule of law; such rhetoric is not found in colonial Korea. In the colony there was neither the separation of the three branches of power nor a constitution that protected basic human rights; thus in the colony the rule of law could not serve as the basis of such criticism. However, in the case of migrant Koreans who lived under the same legal jurisdiction as the Japanese they recognized more vividly the discrimination they experienced as a minority and were demanding equal application of the law. In the passages quoted above the term "the country of the rule of law" appears again and again. Even if we take into account that it might have been emphasized for a

21 Ueundongcheonin, "Daepaneun mubeop cheonji? (Is Osaka a lawless universe?)," *Minjung Sibo*, Inaugural edition, June 15, 1935. The emphasis is mine.

22 "Joseonin e daehan ganje songhwaneul danyeon pyejihara! Geu pyehaeneun makdaehada!! (Stop the deportation of Koreans! The injuries caused are great!!)" *Minjung Sibo*, September 15, 1935. The emphasis is mine.

23 Ueundongcheonin. See footnote #21. The emphasis is mine.

rhetorical impact, or to highlight the discrimination, prejudice, injustice, and violence that migrant Koreans experienced on a daily basis, it is still significant that these writers are knocking on the doors of *naeji* legal system. There was the reality of the lawlessness and policelessness in Japan which turned a blind eye to Koreans "to die" on their own. But Koreans in Japan also saw that the access to law that would "save lives" was not completely off the map; the entrance was close enough to move their power of desire toward that direction. If *naeji* migrant Koreans occupied a ground that was different from the ground Koreans in the colony occupied, their site probably has to be found in this vicinity.

4. From "hole" to "hole"

Migrant Korean communities in the metropole had a characteristic that distinguished them from Korean migrant communities in other places. In Japan, they were formed sporadically not too far from indigenous Japanese communities, which was decidedly different from migrant Korean communities established in the Russian Far East or Northeast China, where migrant Koreans often formed their own community over a vast stretch of land, in isolation from the indigenous population, and often having administrative autonomy.[24] It could possibly be argued that the migrant Korean communities in Japan were part of Japanese society. However, typically, a Korean community in Japan was not assimilated. Instead, Koreans formed small and large settlements within close proximity to the indigenous Japanese populations, and they were typically separate and independent from Japanese society.

Of course, the lines of independence were not the result of active self-affirmation by Koreans but the result of exclusions and

24 See TONOMURA Masaru, op. cit., 118.

segregations by society at large in Japan. Thus, Korean communities in Japan were mostly formed in the vicinity of large construction projects, in slum neighborhoods, or in other areas aversion.[25] Among these, the communities in urban slum neighborhoods, in particular, deserve special attention for they are important for us to gain a sense of these places as historical sites of *naeji* migrant Koreans during the colonial/imperial period.

One such place, as reported by JANG Hyeok-ju from the mid-1930s, was located within 20-30 minutes of one-yen taxi ride from the Ginza district in Tokyo. Unlike in the East End, the slum neighborhood in London, this slum neighborhood was not so dangerous, and "ladies in high heels and western suits, or a leisured woman" would "soon realize that the people there are the same as our readers if they could only withstand the odd gazes of the residents there."[26] Jang visited Tsukimimachi (月見町) in the Shibaura district to report on the leading Korean settlement in the Tokyo area, and he found the settlement formed along the lodging quarters of the longshoremen working in the nearby Shibaura harbor. Where a coal warehouse used to stand, Korean migrant workers built make-shift huts with wood boards and tin roofing. The number of huts kept increasing, and the existing huts were extended. By 1937, approximately six hundred Koreans were living there. Jang's real-life experience of reporting on this story as a journalist was decisive in later developing the story "Golmokgil" (Alleyway) (*Kaizo* 1938. 10).

The protagonist of "Golmokgil" is HEO Jin, a man who threw

25 It was well known that Korean communities in Japan were formed out of exclusion and alienation, and so from the Japanese perspective they contained elements of threat. Thus, for example, the thousands of Korean workers who lived as a collective and worked in a gravel quarry in Tamagawa, near Tokyo, were sometimes portrayed as if they were developing a Korean colony in Japan. "Teito Chikakuni Chosenno Shokuminchi?? Tamagawaberino Senjin Buraku (A Korean Colony near the Capital of Japan?? A Korean Village of Tamagawa Riverside)," *Keijonippo*, 1933. 7. 30.

26 CHANG Hyeok-ju, "Ruporutaju Chosenjin Shurakuwo Iku (Reportage: the Korean Settlements)," *Kaizo*, 1937. 6, 47.

himself in worker's movement in the past but who has since renounced the cause. In the story, the newspaper he publishes, *Donga Sinbo*, is forcibly closed down, but he does not collaborate with his former comrades KIM Sam-dal and AHN Kyung-hee, who now support the imperial policy of assimilating Koreans. Instead, the protagonist maintains his relationship with Korean migrants in the Shibaura settlement. He frequents the settlement there, giving help to day laborers who are unfairly treated by their employers. Kaneda—a Korean who runs an illicit brewery, deals with stolen goods, runs a gambling den, and is involved in loan sharking—is owed money from Sun-yeong. She is about to be sold off to pay for her debt, and Heo Jin saves her and asks her to marry him. At the outset, the relationship between the protagonist and the Korean migrant workers in the settlement smacks teacher-student relationship. However, in comparison to Kim Sam-dal, Heo Jin is a character who tries to accept Koreans "as they are." It is Ahn Kyung-hee, one who collaborates with Kim, the turncoat, who really believes that Koreans are ignorant and uncivilized and therefore must be enlightened.

> ... Once they are back from their work, they will soon drink, start gambling, suddenly get upset and start screaming their heads off: Whaaa.... They don't think about the consequences, and they become violent. When you think about all these things, what can save them is not the movement we were immersed in in the past. I feel that we must find something more immediate and visible. Mr. Kim has said that his idea of establishing Gyopunghoe (an association –Tr.) came from such a thought. Japanification of Korean settlers is just a starting point. In other words, the idea is to improve living standards by relying on government help. The shanty houses must go... I heard the city has a plan to build apartment-style houses.
>
> ......
>
> Unlike the movement we were involved in in the past, Mr. Kim's movement is entirely in line with government policies. What he is demand- ing is that [Koreans] receive exactly the same treatment as Japanese. He began a new movement, and it is the most rational movement. Don't you think this is the most appropriate and effective way to save those people? Especially now?[27]

27 CHANG Hyeok-ju, "Roji (Alleyway)," *Kaizo*, 1938. 10, 26-27. The emphasis is mine.

Kim Sam-dal represents those who want to "improve" the lives of Koreans in *naeji* by being included in the *naeji* world of law, as we have examined before. This "most rational movement," whose purpose was to bring Koreans into the "civilized state" under the Imperial grace of "universal benevolence" demanded in return "*gyopung*," or "rectification of customs." In order to receive the redemption of being a "human inside the legal system" and be treated as an equal to Japanese, Koreans must rid themselves of the tell-tale signs of their savageness. Heo Jin acknowledges that one cannot but recognize the truth in what Kim and others like him say, but at the same time he cannot help but feeling resistant against such an idea, and he feels unsettled about it. By choosing Sun-yeong rather than Ahn Kyung-hee, he wants to have a new beginning. Heo Jin does have a longing for the "wide road" on the other side of the workers' settlement which he believes would make "even this shabby, dark, and disorderly clutter of the settlement look friendly," and he does thus take Sun-yeong out of the settlement and they move to Ganda together. However, he also shows a strong attachment to the world of the narrow "alleyways" of the settlement. "Although ugly and tumor-like, the settlement was still a home in his heart."[28]

Thus in the story "Golmokgil" the author is hesitant about the assimilation argument, and through the protagonist the author shows a strong attachment to the lives of the people in the settlement. Could it be that the author became privy to certain irreducible reality of Korean communities in Japan when, as a journalist earlier, he reported on one such settlement? He witnessed first-hand the terrible conditions of the apartment buildings that the local government proposed to build in the place of the Korean settlement,[29] but that was not the only reason for his hesitance.

28 Ibid., 17.

29 See CHANG Hyeok-ju, "Ruporutaju Chosenjin Shurakuwo Iku (Reportage: the Korean Settlements)," 51-52.

The Tsukimimachi Korean settlement in Shibaura, which became the background for Jang's story, was located in an area that was easily accessible by anyone, but finding the entrance to go inside the settlement was another matter. Jang was lost for a long time before he was helped by several Korean women to find it.

> An irregular hole had its mouth gaped open, and I went in as if being sucked in. And indeed, it was the passageway to the settlement. Perhaps it was the only passageway. Between planks of wood and columns, it was barely wide enough for one person to go through. Taking a peek inside the houses through small crevices, I could see a raw straw mat or a wet and dirty tatami mattress on which children or adults were sleeping wrapped in blankets made of red and white cloth from Joseon or black Japanese fabric. A fly would be buzzing over the child's mouth, as if making a surveillance flight. A few steps from there, the hole became dark. One then noticed, there were houses or a laundry drying rack hanging across the alleyway and covering up the sky. [...] From one hole to another hole, this was the alleyway of the settlement. An ant house, or earthworm tunnels suddenly came to my mind. This hole was a tunnel connecting one house after another, or rather one room after another.[30]

Jang Hyeokju had to find the "hole" in order to go inside the settlement. Inside this hole was a narrow and dark tunnel that connected yet smaller holes. The imagery of an ant house as the Korean migrant workers' settlement, not too far from the heart of Tokyo, the capital of the empire, symbolizes how *oeji* exists inside *naeji*. The outer territory inside the inner territory is the sphere of the extra-legal people who live inside the sphere of the law of the inner territory, and as such it exists like a gaping hole. The hole reveals in an "invisible way" the presence of a system that is based on discrimination and gap between the *naeji* and *oeji*. This is not to say that the colony and the empire—between which the "hole" that was the migrant Korean community existed—were actual entities themselves. The colony and the empire appear as if they have actual—that is corporeal—indices of territorial, ethnic (national), and linguistic identity/difference.

30 Ibid., 48-49.

However, the identity/difference in each of these categories is the identity/difference that is (re)produced by the colonial/imperial regime. Accordingly, this hole is not visible in the dominant discursive field where opposing concepts, such as Joseon vs. Japan, resistance vs. pro-Japan, and nation vs. class, constantly clashed; and it exists not so much "between" the colony and the empire, but it pierces through "inside" the colonial/imperial regime in a non-homogeneous manner.

The hole is the historical site of the *naeji* Korean migrants; it (non)existed as a hole in the imperial legal system, a hole in the assimilationism, a hole in the Asianism; as such it reveals the limits of the colonial/imperial regime in the very urban vicinity of the metropole. Of course, the discovery of the limits of this regime is possible, only when one finds the hole in a firurative sense. In the case of Jang Hyeok-ju, he seems to have found the hole in the literal sense only, surveying the workers' settlement for a report and even naming it as "a hole" himself. At least in this story he seems to be doubtful as to whether or not the "realistic and rational" movement to assimilate Koreans in Japan could fill up this irreducible hole and create a single homogeneously level "board."[31]

5. Our Muslim, Or the Place of a Mysterious Bug

Kim Sam-dal's argument for Japanification of *naeji* Koreans in "Golmokgil" takes place with ethnic discrimination and disparity in the background. Here the disparity between *naeji* Koreans and Japanese is translated as the difference between "a mere life" and "more than a mere life." Nevertheless, HEO Jin hesitates, not

31 However, not too long after the publication of "Golmokgil" Jang published his infamous article "Chosenno Chisikijinni Uttaeru (Appealing to Korean intellectuals)" (*Bungei*, 1939. 2), in which he argues for complete assimilation of Koreans. The instability and inconsistency in Jang's personal political views are beyond the scope of this study, and the subject requires a separate discussion.

readily agreeing to expurgating the animal-like life, nor quite affirming it. He observed and described the "hole" with sympathy, but he could not willingly embrace the life inside. Thus Sun-yeong was chosen from the hole but she had to be rescued from there.

To better understand the life inside the hole, let us now go through "Beollae" (insect) (*Sinjo*, July 1941) by KIM Sa-ryang.[32] In this story, "I" am the protagonist story who studies painting even as he lives as a ragman. This lonely and lonesome protagonist has a friend in a morphine-addicted old man called "*Jigimi*." A self-professed soldier from the time of the old Korea, he goes around the neighborhood always muttering 'Jigimi!' (a mild expletive -Tr.), and so it became his name. In the Shibaura harbor, "the Mecca and Medina of Korean migrant workers"[33] a ship, loaded with coal, comes in every morning. Most of the day laborers unloading the coal and cleaning the bottom of the ship are Koreans, and most of these workers consider Jigimi a screwball and an imbecile; they think of him as "a despicable man whose existence the world has never once needed;"[34] in other words, they treat him as if he is an insect. Nevertheless, at the dawn of every morning when the ship comes in Jigimi goes around *hamba* waking up the workers. "I" paint this Jigimi. In the meantime, one day, a Korean university student, who would break into a wail while citing statistics that revealed the wretchedness of the lives of the Korean workers in Japan, suddenly came to work at the harbor as a stevedore. He promptly became sick after one day of work and becomes mad. The workers collect money among themselves and send the student back to Joseon when they found a man travelling back to the student's old home

32 "Beollae" was published in Japanese. It is the modified version of "Jigimi," which was published in Korean in *Samcheolli*, 1941. 4.

33 KIM Sa-ryang (1973), "Mushi (A Bug)" in *Kim Sa-ryang Zenshu* (The complete works of Kim Sa-ryang), Vol. II, Kawadeshoboshinsha, 8.

34 Ibid., 10.

village. However, on this day too, saying that he cannot wake up workers if he goes back home, Jigimi is waking up workers at the crack of the dawn when the ship comes in.

In this story, there are four main types of characters; they are the protagonist "I," Jigimi, the university student, and the workers. In terms of proximity to the workplace, at one end is the protagonist and the student, and at the other end the workers. Although "I" am a rag picker, the fact that "I" dream of becoming a painter and that "I" have no particular relationship with the workers put "me" at the opposite end of the workers. Also, just as the university student has placed the abstraction device of statistics between himself and reality,[35] "I" too want to install the representational device of painting between "myself" and reality. The devices that "I" and the student have are a kind of translation device. It is dangerous to engage directly with reality without this device, as was illustrated by the breakdown of the student who went for stevedoring for one morning. Thus, "I" with the translation device on the one hand, and the workers who are on the other side of the device, on the other, never mix a word together throughout this story. The only character who mixes words with "me" and the workers alike is Jigimi, who goes around murmuring utterances that no one can actually understand. He speaks a language that is understood neither in the world of the workers nor on this side of the translation device; as such, he is an Ah Q-like human.[36]

---

35 "... you don't know how sacred the numbers are. See, you are like that. If you are ignorant of numbers, that is, statistics, you are done with. You are out. Me, why, what in the world do you think brought me, myself, here? I am not the struggling kind of student who might be coming by a place like this to supplement his income. Let me have you know, not all university students are the same. You see, I am a student at the social sciences department of XX University, and I pay my own tuition there, in full. That's right, you see, I came here, I came here to get numbers, to have exact statistics!" Ibid., 18.

36 See HWANG Ho-deok (2011), "Jeguk Ilbon gwa beonyeok (eomneun) jeongchi (Japan the empire and politics of (without) translation)," in *Beollae wa Jeguk* (A bug and the empire), Saemulgyeol.

However, what is interesting is that although Jigimi is a bug, or because he is a bug, his position is similar to that of a deity.

> The moaning of the steam engine could be heard from every direction, and the sound of foghorns pierced through the darkness from near and far. Looking at him in this light, Jigimi is like a prophet, or a god, who has control over everything. So, if we could call Shibaura the Mecca or the Medina of Korean migrants, perhaps we can then call him God [Allah] of the sacred text [Quoran], because he is indeed a man of eternal solitude "who has not begotton [anyone] nor is begotton from [anyone] (生まず, 生まれず)," and "there is no one who is comparable" as there is only one such person in *trailokya* (three worlds -Tr.).[37]

In the last sentence of the story "Beollae," the author comments that the "image of Jigimi jumping up and down to welcome" the barge coming into the harbor "was as beautiful as a Muslim basked in the evening glow of a setting sun and praying."[38] Here again we can see that Jigimi has a metaphorical reference point in a Muslim. Here, a deity, the only begotton son of God, is an orphan all alone in the world; and he who is the lowliest and he who is the most exalted are equal in that they are both incomparable to any other being. In short, both the bug and deity are exceptional beings that exist outside of the boundary of law and order. Kim Sa-ryang uses this notion the bug, and the Muslim as the exotic, as a cipher denoting *naeji* migrant Koreans.[39] In fact, it seems that around this time Kim Sa-ryang often used the code "beollae" to refer to *naeji* migrant Koreans. For example, MURAYAMA Tomoyoshi's theatre group Shinkyo

37 Kim Sa-ryang, "Mushi (Bug)," 13.

38 Ibid., 22.

39 In a letter exchanged between Kim Sa-ryang and Kim Dalsu, this analogy is made more direct. When Kim Dalsu sends an invitation to Kim Sa-ryang to attend a "sports day," a festival of friendly sports competitions, for Koreans in Yokosuka, which is where Kim Dalsu was staying, Kim Sa-ryang replies "I will be certain to attend the sports day for 'Muslims and bugs.'" (KIM Dal-soo, "Senshisita KIM Sa-ryang (KIM Sa-ryang Killed in Battle)," *Shinnihonbungaku*, 1952. 12, 51) Kim Sa-ryang later portrayed the event and the people he met there in "Oyakata Gobse (The Hunchback Foreman)" (*Shincho*, 1942. 1).

was preparing to stage a play written by Kim Sa-ryang when its members were arrested and the group was forcibly disbanded by the authorities in Japan (August 1940). No copy of the script is extant to verify all relevant details, but the title of the play the group was preparing to stage was "Fushigina Mushi [不思議な虫]" (A mysterious bug), which had been translated as such from the Korean title of the same play "Bulgasari" (Starfish).[40] Those who live in the "hole" that Jang Hyeok-ju encountered in his report are captured by Kim Sa-ryang in the imagery insect and Muslim as exceptional beings.

Jigimi is a schizophrenic figure whose bearings would instantaneously be as "gallantly dignified"[41] as a soldier but who would just as soon collapse in tears when "I" scolded him. His speech, from the viewpoint of a "language," was broken, and it was difficult to tell what structural order it was following. Thus while it stretched over the world of the workers and the world on this side of the translation device, it could not be reduced to the language of one or the other world. Like the "hole," it is precisely this aspect of Jigimi that makes it possible to consider him as an allegory of *naeji* migrant Koreans during this period. Furthermore, the two worlds contrasted in "Beollae" are the world of the workers, on one hand, and the world on "this" side of the translation device, on the other; in terms of the two layers of life referred to earlier, the former can be seen as an imagery "a mere life" and the latter as the imagery of "more than a mere life."[42] There was nothing extraneous or ornamental in the lives

40 *Yomiuri Shinbun*, December 22, 1939, Evening Edition, p. 3. Quoted in Gwak Hyeong-deok, "Gim Sa-ryang ui Ilbon mundan debwi eseobuteo 'Gomesinte' sidaeggaji (1939-1942) (From Kim Sa-ryang's literary debut in Japan to the 'Gomesinte" era (1939-1942))," in *Kim Sa-ryang, Jakpumgwa Yeongu 2* (Kim Sa-ryang, His works and studies 2), KIM Jae-yong and GWAK Hyeong-deok editors and translators, Yeokrak, 2009, 643. Also, MURAYAMA Tomoyoshi remembers the title as 'Fushigina Mushi (A mysterious insect).' MURAYAMA Tomoyoshi, "KIM Sa-ryangwo Omou (Remembering KIM Sa-ryang)," *Shinnihonbungaku*, 1952. 12, 55.

41 Kim Sa-ryang, "Mushi (Bug)," 22.

42 This is not to say that this author believes that the world of labor is that of "a mere

of the workers who slept in *hamba*, forty or so of them sleeping in a ten-*cho* room, or a room big enough to fit only ten *tatami* mattresses, and waking up almost automatically to the sound of a ship arriving at the harbor and working all day unloading it. They ate, they worked, and they slept. In contrast, the lives of the protagonist "I" and the university student were supplemented by painting and statistics, a device, or a means, that disallowed their lives to become "a mere life." However, these supplementary means could only be sustained when they were used to make an abstraction out of the immediacy of the animal-like lives of the workers.

In the colonial/imperial regime where discrimination was institutionalized, the way to keep *naeji* Koreans in the place of their everyday life was to keep "a mere life" and "more than a mere life" apart. The difference between the two lives was the dynamic force that transformed the fear of the former into an incentive to strive for the latter. The violence that drove *naeji* migrant Koreans to live "a mere life," that drove them to animal-like deaths, further accelerated this transformation. Thousands of Koreans had already met animal-like deaths in the wake of the Great Kanto Earthquake as they embodied this difference and "exceptionality;" and the "independent communities" of *naeji* migrant Korean workers, the result of exclusion and expulsion, often shared the same characteristics as a concentration camp.[43]

life" but that within the narrative structure of this story it is portrayed as such.

43 For example, individual Korean workers who tried to escape from their subhuman labor conditions were hunted down and lynched ("Ilbon nodongjadan Joseonineul nanta (A group of Japanese workers beat Koreans)," *Donga Ilbo*, April 22, 1920. In the case of dam construction workers in the remote mountain region of Nigata, a large number of Korean workers were lynched and murdered ("Ilbon eseo Joseoin dae haksal (Massacre of Koreans in Japan)," *Donga Ilbo*, August 1, 1922; "Sinseokhyeon sageon teukjeon: Hakdae chamhyeongui sillye (Special report on the Niigata-ken incident: An actual case of a cruel decapitation)," *Donga Ilbo*, August 20, 1922.) Also, there were cases in which an entire Korean community was forcibly relocated ("Daepan Joseonin gangje ijeon (Osaka Koreans forcibly relocated)," *Chosun Ilbo*, November 1, 1029). Yet in another case, Japanese workers attacked a Korean village in order to destroy a labor dispute involving Koreans ("Joseonin chollakeul seupgyeok,

Ethnic discrimination did not simply make a value judgment on ethnic differences; it drove people's lives into animal-like "mere life."

However, if we compare the space that Jigimi inhabits in "Beollae" in the context of the exceptional space occupied by the migrant Koreans who are wedged between "a mere life" and "more than a mere life, the singularity of their place revealed; this singularity cannot be reduced entirely to the operational principles of the colonial/imperial regime. Like many migrant Koreans who lived in flux as a lumpen proletarian, Jigimi is unable to enter the workers' world but instead hovers around it. Nor does he have any device to translate himself or the reality around him into an abstract language. More than anything else, he is a schizophrenic who speaks a language that cannot be understood in either world but who still has dealings in both worlds. In fact, the Korean migrants' society was a society of Korean language within the society of "Kokugo (national language)," or Japanese, and at the same time it was not the society of Korean language, or at least not the standard Korean language. When they spoke Japanese, it was as if they were speaking "Japanese patched from everywhere,"[44] or they spoke in their own Japanese dialect which consisted of "dialects from all over the country mixed with standard Japanese and working class dialect."[45] When they spoke in Korean, they mumbled in "jumbled up Korean."[46]

Thus, the Koreans in Japan, the outsiders of the inner territory, were the exceptional beings in both *naeji* and *oeji*; as such they

gaok 11 gando pagoe (Korean village attacked, 11 house units destroyed)," *Chosun Ilbo*, May 24, 1932).

44 CHANG Hyeok-ju, "Yushujinsei (Melancholy Life)," *Nihonhyoron*, 1937. 10, 443.

45 Ibid., 449.

46 KIM Sa-ryang, "Mukyuikka (A Hibiscus Family)" (*Kaizo*, 1940. 9), *Kim Sa-ryang Zenshu*, Vol. 1, Kawadeshoboshinsha, 1973, 176.

existed as insects, as Muslims, inside the hole that pierced through the colonial/imperial regime, the hole that represented the limits of the colonial/imperial regime. It is not surprising, in a certain sense, that they remained as "invisible people" in the world of law, language, and order. However, when there is an upheaval in the colonial/imperial regime, and when there is an agitation in the nation-state regime, these "invisible people" reveal where the limits are in the regime and become visible themselves.

Naeji Koreans suffered from the constant fear and anxiety of having to live "a mere life." Granted that they existed in a hole in the colonial/imperial regime, their lives were still extremely precarious; they were perpetually exposed to the possibility of being disavowed semantically, ontologically, and biologically. Even if they could disentangle themselves from the political-economic discrimination, which was the basic engine of the colonial/imperial regime, theirs was a place that could not be free of worries about violence.

I began this paper with a scene from *Mansejeon* in which I pointed out that YI In-hwa, the student, never encountered *yobos*, the Korean workers from farming villages. I also pointed out that it was while crossing Hyeonhaetan that YI identifies himself with the *yobos* in a bitter awakening of an ethnic sentiment. In Japan he could not meet Korean workers there, and when he visited Korea he would soon go back to Japan repeating to himself, "It's a grave here, a grave with maggots swarming around!" It is significant that this YI In-hwa becomes aware of the workers' presence aboard a ship crossing the sea. It is not simply because Hyeonhaetan is the border between *naeji* and *oeji* that YI In-hwa has an epiphany in which he identifies himself ethnically with the Korean migrant workers, and with tenant farmers of Korea by extension. It is because Hyeonhaetan was not simply a border but a bluff inside the colonial/imperial regime at the edge of which he could not but become aware of his ethnicity, class, and gender in fear, anxiety, and danger. However, because this awakening is accompanied by fear and anxiety, YI In-hwa does not meet the *yobos* on the ship face to face even as he identifies himself with them as having the same nationality. To understand structurally this absence of encounter between those whose migration hinged upon a premise of repatriation, on the one hand, and the peasant *yobos* whose lives were uprooted, on the other, we must start from examining the limitations inside the colonial/imperial regime where the uprooted knocked about.

Bibliography

1. References

CHANG Hyeok-ju (1937. 6), "Ruporutaju Chosenjin Shurakuwo Ink (Reportage: the Korean Settlements)," *Kaizo*.

______________ (1937. 10), "Yushujinsei (Melancholy Life)," *Nihonhyoron*.

______________ (1938. 10), "Roji (Alleyway)," *Kaizo*.

Chosun Ilbo, Donga Ilbo, Minjung Sibo, Gyeongseong Ilbo, Sin Ilbon Munhak.

KIM Sa-ryang (1973), *Kim Sa-ryang Zenshu* (The Complete Works of Kim Sa-ryang), Vol. I·II, Kawadeshoboshinsha.

YOM Sang-seop (1987), "Mansejeon" (The manse story) in *Yeom Sangseop jeonjip* (The complete works of Yeom Sang-seop) 1, Mineumsa.

2. Papers and Books

ASANO Toyomi (2008), *Teikoku Nihon no Shokuminchi Housei* (The Colonial Legislative System of Imperial Japan), Nagoya University Press.

HWANG Ho-deok (2011), "Jeguk Ilbon gwa beonyeok (eom-neun) jeongchi" (Japan the empire and politics of (with-out) translation), in *Beollae wa Jeguk* (A bug and the empire), Saemulgyeol.

KAJIMURA Hideki (1993), "8 · 15 izenno Zainichi Chosenjin no Rekishi (The History of Zainichi Koreans until 8 · 15)," *Collected Works of Kajimura Hideki*, Vol. 6, Akashi-shoten.

KEN Kawashima (2009), "Sangpumhwa, bulhwakjeongseong, geu-rigo junggan chakchwi: Jeongangi Ilbonui maknodong sijangeseo ui Joseonin nodongjadeul ui tujaeng" (Com-modification, Contingency and Intermediary Exploitation: Korean Proletarian Struggles in the Day Labor Market of Interwar Japan) in Henry EM and GWAK Jun-hyeok eds. *Geundaeseong ui yeokseol: Hangukhak gwa Ilbonhak ui gyeonggye reul neomeo (Entangled modernities: Crossings Between Korean and Japanese Studies)*, Humanitas.

KIM Chan-jeong (2010), *Kankoku Heigo Hyakunen to Zainichi* (100 years of Korea-Japan Annexation and Zainichi), Shinchosha.

KIM Gwang-yeol (2001), "Jeongan gi Ilbon dohang Joseoninui teukjil" (The characteristics of Koreans crossing over to Japan during the war time) in *Ilbonhakbo*, No. 46.

______________ (2009), "Jaeil Haninui minjok haebang undong gwa 3.1 undong ginyeom" (National liberation movements waged by Koreans in Japan and their commemoration of the March 1st Movement) in *Hanguk geunhyeondaesa yeongu* (The study of Korean modern and contemporary history), Vol. 50.

______________ (2010), *Haninui Ilbon ijusa yeongu: 1910-1940-nyeondae* (A study of the migration history of Koreans migrating to Japan: 1910-1940s), Nonhyeong.

KIM In-deok (1996), *Sikminji sidae Jaeil Joseonin undong yeongu* (A study of the movement of the Koreans in Janpan during the colonial time), Gukhak Jaryowon.

__________ (1996), "1920-nyeondae huban jaeil Joseoninui saenghwal sangtae yeongu (A study of everyday living conditions of Koreans in Japan in the latter half of the 1920s) in *Hanguk geunhyeondaesa yeongu* (The study of Korean modern and contemporary history), Vol. 5.

OZAKI Hideki (1991), *Kindai Bungaku no Shokon* (The Scars of Modern Literature), Iwanamishoten.

SAKAI Naoki (2003), translation by YI Gyu-su in *Gungminjuui ui poiesis* (The *poiesis* of nationalism), Changbi.

SIN Ji-yeong (2011), "'Daedonga Munhakja Daehoe' raneun munbeop, geu byeonhyeong gwa janyeodeul" (The grammar called "The Greater East Asia Conference of Literati:" Its metamorphosis and residues) in *Hanguk munhak yeongu* (The study of Korean literature), Vol. 40.

SUGIHARA Toru (1998), *Ekkyosuru Tami: Kindai Osakano Chosenjinshi Kenkyu* (Border-crossing People: A Study of Korean's History in Modern Osaka), Shinkansha.

TONOMURA Masaru, translated by SIN Yu-won and KIM Indeok (2010), *Jaeil Joseonin sahoeui yeoksahakjeok yeongu* (A historical study of the community of Koreans in Japan), Nonhyeong.

YI Seung-il (2008), *Joseon Chongdokbu beopje jeongchaek* (The legislative policy of Chosen Government-General), Yeoksa bipyeongsa.

2

The Japan-China Friendship Center and Sino-Japanese Relations:

A Battle of Allegiances to A Nation-state and A Cold-War Bloc

by KWON Heok-tae

SungKongHoe University

Department of Japanese Studies

1. Introduction

The Cold War was a military confrontation between socialism and capitalism in which a diplomatic, political, and cultural alliance along an ideological category formed one "bloc" and was pitted against another such "bloc." The Cold War bloc logic entailed anti-Communism, targeting the Union of Soviet Socialist Republics (the Soviet Union) and the People's Republic of China, on the one hand, and anti-Americanism and anti-Capitalism on the other. 'Anti-' always accompanied 'pro-' in the military logic, and this acquired internal stability with repression from above and acquiescence from below. A bloc is of course a single unit. However, this unit is also a union, or a federation, of smaller base units, or nation-states. Furthermore, although a bloc pledges a certain ideological unity as such, it does not necessarily contain the self-logic of aiming at the dissolution of nation-states and the building of a "world-state."

Logically then, at times, the bloc-logic and the nation-state-logic would be congruent, but at other times they would contradict each other. In other words, the Cold War was a confrontation between socialist and capitalist 'blocs,' not necessarily 'nations.' Socialism and capitalism are not nations, and thus the confrontation between socialism and capitalism is manifested through a confrontation between individual nations belonging to their respective blocs.

Of course, a hierarchical order existed within each bloc, with the United States and the Soviet Union at the top of their respective poles. However, this hierarchy did not necessarily imply the dissolution of nation-states; to be exact, it was built upon the premise of the existence of nation-states. Given this condition, a bloc-logic and a nation-state-logic were frequently doused in a relationship of potential tension.

Accordingly, when a bloc tries to liquidate a nation-state, or when political changes within a nation-state contradict the bloc logic—and as long as such political changes do not presuppose the dissolution of the nation-state—the nation-state in question theoretically has the possibility of transferring its allegiance to the other bloc.

It is this aspect of the Cold War structure in Asia that is particularly different from Europe, the original home of the Cold War. In Asia, and in the Third World, whether or not to join a Cold War bloc was a question that was posed simultaneously and in parallel with the question of national liberation (independence) from colonial powers; thus, there is always the possibility the logic of a nation-state theoretically overpowering the Cold

War logic. Accordingly, while the Cold War logic within a bloc is important for understanding Asia or the Third World, the influence of the bloc logic is not so absolute that it always overpowers the nation-state logic. For this reason, in examining the Cold War in Asia, one has to take into consideration the relationship—congruities and incongruities—between the bloc and the nation-state. This is the first problematic framing this paper.

The second problematic is related to the first, but it has to do with the possibility of division or conflict within a Cold-War bloc. The root of this particular problematic lies in the fact that in Asia, or in the Third World more broadly, the universality of socialist or capitalist ideology could not fully take the nation-state logic under its wings. The dispute between the People's Republic of China and the Soviet Union had the appearance of an ideological fight over divergent socialist paths. In actuality it illustrated the utter ineffectiveness of Soviet-led Cold War logic in Asia when its ideology conflicted with a nation-state pursuing its autonomy and independence.

The disavowal of the exclusive leadership of Soviet socialism in North Korea and Vietnam is a good example. The example of the historical conflict between the Japanese Communist Party (JCP) and the Communist Party of China (CCP), the main focus of this paper, is also an example of how difficult it was for Soviet-led socialism and its universality to take root in Asia.

The Cold War is still an entrenched system in Asia in the aftermath of its collapse in the West because the logic of national liberation = nation-statehood is still strong in the Cold War logic in Asia. This is why it is important to introduce the history of intra-bloc conflict in the study of the history of the Cold War in Asia.

Third, the particular aspect of the Cold War in Asia as described above served as the background for the "hot wars" fought in Asia and the Third World vis-a-vis the Cold War fought in Europe. The Korean and Vietnam Wars, which involved struggles for achieving socialism and national liberation simultaneously, are leading examples Asian hot wars vis-a-vis the European Cold War. This is why it is important to examine how the European Cold War was structurally enmeshed with the "hot wars" in Asia and the Third World.

Fourth, in contrast to the Cold War structure in Europe, which was relatively free from the burdens of history, such as wars and invasions, in the Third World, and in particular in Asia, the legacy of colonialism had a strong influence in the formation of the Cold War structure. For example, while Germany was active in breaking with its fascist past, Japan was quite passive in renouncing its colonial history. The burden of history was not limited to the post-war Japanese attitude. The cause of the negative influence of colonialism in post-war Asia can be found, first and foremost, in the fact that the winners and losers of the war did not quite tally up, and in how the Allies, in particular the U.S., handled Japan. But the more important cause lies in the fact that Asia was thoroughly excluded in the post-war reconstruction process of Japan.

Fifth, there is the issue of separating state ideology from civil society (the civilian sector). In other words, formal confrontation between states does not necessarily preemptively exclude all civilian exchanges (with the exception of the China-Taiwan and North-South Korean cases). Accordingly, one has to examine seriously the role of civil society and its relative autonomy vis-a-vis the state. At the same time, however, one has to also take into consideration that exclusively civilian exchanges have a limited role and that they do not constitute a factor determining a formal state confrontation.

Keeping in mind these five problematics, I examine in this paper the Japan-China Friendship Center in Tokyo, which had been the stronghold of the China-Japan friendship movement in Japan. Originally, the Friendship Center was built in Tokyo in the 1930s in order to control and supervise Manchukuo students studying in Japan. After the war, a serious of confrontations took place regarding its ownership and the right to use its facilities. In the 1950s, confrontations took place between the Japanese government and Chinese-Japanese[#], and in the 1960s between the Japanese Communist Party and Chinese-Japanese. Since the normalization of relations between the PRC and Japan in 1972, the Friendship Center has served as the stronghold for PRC-Japan friendship while the ownership dispute was put on hold. The purpose of this paper is to reconstruct the history of post-war China-Japan relations by focusing on the various controversies that took place regarding the Center's facilities.

2. The Normalization of PRC-Japan Diplomatic Relations and the "Reversal" of the Cold War Structure

> The restoration of diplomatic relations with China will eventually be realized. It will be realized in the not too-distant future. In any case the times have changed. The threat of war has not completely disappeared, but for the time being it is distant, and even I, the pessimist that I am, cannot but recognize that. Furthermore, there is the U.S. approval, and the business sector has already authorized it. [...] Even though the meaning [of the normalization of diplomatic relations—author] has been altered, it is better than to not normalize relations at all. That is natural [...] however, we have to at least remember in our hearts that the conscience of the people of Japan is not expressed, and that ultimately the normalization of diplomatic relations between China and Japan has not been realized in a form in which we can expect solidarity between the peoples of China and Japan to take place in

---

In this paper, the author uses the term huaqiao (華僑) to refer to the Chinese population at large, including those from the mainland, Taiwan, and former Manchukuo, residing permanently in Japan. The term is translated here mainly as 'Chinese-Japanese.' Along with it, other terms, such as 'Chinese residents of Japan,' and 'overseas Chinese,' are used interchangeably, where appropriate -Tr.

accordance with that conscience. (August, 1972)[1]

I was really curious about the success or failure of the meeting. When the signing ceremony was delayed, I even felt a bad omen... As the Joint Statement was being read, point by point, my shoulders sank further and further. It was almost what I had expected, no it was beyond what I had expected. Frankly, the impression I have is that it was beyond what I could have imagined. Perhaps the Chinese victims cannot rest in peace, but at least the Japanese war victims will now perhaps rest in peace. (November, 1972)[2]

Takeuchi Yoshimi, the leading post-war thinker and sinologist in Japan, published articles shortly before and after the normalization of PRC-Japan diplomatic relations (September 1972), from which the above two quotations are taken. In an article published in March 1960,[3] he assumes that PRC-Japan diplomatic relations would be normalized based on Japanese acknowledgment of its war crime responsibilities. When the normalization of relations suddenly arrived in September 1972, it seems that he accepted it with mixed feelings. Upon hearing about the first PRC nuclear test that took place on October 16, 1964 he lamented that it was "an unfortunate event. It should not have happened, and it should not be allowed to happen. As a human being, and as Japanese, there will be few who would not regret this event." Thus, he did not hide his disappointment with the PRC. But he also said, "outside of the realm of reason, and speaking from the gut, it is difficult to say so, but in one's heart one cannot help feel that it is a job well done. I cannot hide this sense of pride that they snubbed the Anglo-Saxons and their lackeys (Japanese included)" (January, 1965).[4] In other words, Takeuchi also accepted the PRC nuclear test as an event that symbolized the PRC's

1 Takeuchi (1980-82), "Chûgoku wo shiru tame ni" (To understand china) (Number 98), *Takeuchi Yoshimi zenshû* (Collected works of Takeuchi Yoshimi), Vol. 11, 142-143.

2 Ibid., "Ichi hyaku ichi, meiwaku" (One hundred and one, bewilderment), 160.

3 See for example, Takeuchi (1966), "Sensô sekinin ni tsuite" (On war responsibility), *Nihon to Ajia* (Japan and Asia).

4 Takeuchi (1980-82), "Shû Sakujin kara kaku jikken made" (From Zhou Zuoren to nuclear weapons testing), op. cit. 295.

anti-Westernism/anti-imperialism. Now that the PRC normalized its relations with the U.S. and other countries in the West, and with Japan, the West's underling, it must have been for him a sign of "changing times," a "reversal of values" that "cannot but be accepted." Thus Takeuchi declares "In form, it is not [yet—author] a treaty, but in contents it contains more than what a peace treaty might. My pessimism collapsed fantastically." He added, "For now, I want to congratulate today's achievement. Looking back, it was a long journey. The greatest irrationality has now been eliminated. Or, a path to eliminating the greatest irrationality has been opened. Congratulations are well deserved."[5] He then promptly disbanded the China Conference (中国の会), an organization he had been presiding over, whose aim was the normalization of Japan-China relations. The all too sudden announcement of the normalization of PRC-Japan relations was probably not the only reason why Takeuchi "could not but recognize" "the changing times." Many "pro-China" intellectuals in post-war Japan, Takeuchi included, denounced the Japan-U.S. Security Treaty that was antagonistic toward the Socialist bloc; they supported the "one China" policy and argued that Japan must fully take the war responsibilities as a precondition for normalizing relations with the PRC. However, the PRC-Japan Joint Statement (September 29, 1972), which Takeuchi could not but have mixed feelings about as he watched it being read, ended the "abnormal state" of PRC-Japan relations, recognized the PRC as the only legitimate Chinese government, and acknowledged that Taiwan was part of PRC territory. But according to the statement, the PRC will not seek reparations from Japan, and there was not a word about the Japan-U.S. Security Treaty.

Even among the Japanese New Left, who accepted Maoism not just for Japan but as a universal revolutionary philosophy—amidst

5 Takeuchi (1980-82), "Ichi hyaku ichi, meiwaku" (One hundred and one, bewilderment), op. cit. 163-164.

the whirlwind of controversy surrounding the PRC-Soviet conflict and the Great Cultural Revolution—the "change of heart" on the part of the PRC was perplexing, to say the least. For example Sakaguchi Hiroshi, one of the leaders of the United Red Army who came from the Revolutionary Left Wing, saw on a television screen the scene of Nixon being welcomed by Zhou Enlai as he and other members of the United Red Army were exchanging gunfire with the police in the Asama Sanso incident. He recollects the event as follows: "It was a shocking event that shook the principles of our armed struggle at its very foundation. However, our heads were too immature to understand even a single thread of its background, and all we could do was gaze vacantly at the scene of Nixon visiting China."[6] Kato Michinori, who also saw the same televised scene at Asama Sanso, a holiday lodge, as he and the others were in an armed standoff with the police, remembered that it raised the question of "what are we fighting for?" and that he lost his fighting spirit as a result.[7] Also, Nagata Yoko, the highest-ranking officer to have been tried and sentenced to death, recollected the Nixon visit in her book published in 1990 that she "could not understand what had happened and was thus perplexed."[8]

The Japanese "New Left" criticized Soviet socialism as "Stalinism" or "Socialist imperialism;" its relationship with the Japanese Communist Party was also antagonistic and it was seeking a new form of socialism. For most of the New Left, Mao's socialism was an ally, a living revolutionary path, and the "home" of the revolution indispensable to the overthrowing of the Liberal Democratic Party in Japan and U.S. imperialism. It goes without saying that the Revolutionary Left Wing of the Japanese Communist Party and the Marxist-Leninist Faction of the Japa-

6 Sakaguchi (1993), *Asama sansô 1972* (Part two), 90.

7 Yamadaira (2011), *Rengô sekigun monogatari, kôen* (The story of the United Red Army, red flame), 450.

8 Nagata (1990), *Zoku jûroku no bohyô* (The sixteen gravestones), 89.

nese Revolutionary Communist League, both Maoists, readily embraced Maoist tenets of socialism. But even those who were critical of Chinese socialism among the New Left recognized the validity of the "generation theory" and the logic of "self-negation" in the Great Cultural Revolution and the Red Guards. They even found the presence of the will to "permanent revolution" that they dreamed of in Chinese socialism, which struggled for anti-imperialism and anti-Americanism even as they endured the hardship of isolation from the international community. For all these proponents of the New Left, the People's Republic of China was not a mere nation-state but the revolutionary movement itself. Accordingly, the PRC-US and PRC-Japan normalizations of diplomatic relations created an "intolerable" situation in which their hero took the hands of their archenemy.

On February 26, 1971, with Sohyo, or the General Council of Trade Unions of Japan, the Japan Socialist Party (JSP), which had been at the forefront of Japan-PRC diplomacy, formed the National Conference on the Restoration of China-Japan Diplomatic Relations, and the party made normalization of China-Japan relations the backbone of its foreign policy.[9] Thus it could not but welcome the government's announcement. However, the JSP had been completely excluded from the state-to-state normalization negotiations. Furthermore, it was impossible to find in the Joint Statement any reference to the U.S. as "the common enemy" of the peoples of China and Japan. This was in stark contrast to the statements made jointly by the JSP and the CCP, on numerous occasions of the former visiting latter, denouncing the U.S. as precisely that. The Japanese Communist Party also officially welcomed the normalization announcement. At the same time, however, it also expressed dissatisfaction at the fact that the Joint Statement did not mention the US-Japan Security Treaty and the

9 See Hara (2000), *Sengoshi no naka no Nihon Shakaitô* (The Japan Socialist Party in postwar history).

China-Japan territorial conflict over the Senkaku Islands (Diaoyutai in Chinese). It also did not hide its dissatisfaction about the fact that there was no apology from the CCP about its "unfair intervention in internal affairs"[10] of the JCP. On the whole, except for certain far-right political elements, the Japanese response to the normalization announcement was positive. Even the New Komeito Party (NKP, New Clean Government Party), which had argued for the normalization of Japan-China relations since the 1960s, and who actually played an important role in the intergovernmental normalization dialogue, welcomed the Joint Statement of 1972.

Thus the normalization of China-Japan relations in 1972 was an event in which Japanese conservative forces—which had taken an antagonistic position against the People Republic of China very much in line with the Cold-War stance—held hands with PRC as it welcomed the Joint Statement. On the other hand, the various entities on the left, which had been consistently advocating for improvement of China-Japan relations, were "alienated" from the normalization process. Thus it was an event in which one could read the reversal of Cold-War dynamics. Of course, Takeuchi took this development as a sign of hope, saying that "a door has been opened to eliminate the greatest absurdity" of the fetters (the threat of war) of the Cold War. However, judging from what followed the Joint Statement, one cannot quite say that China-Japan relations broke free from the bondage of the Cold War that Takeuchi spoke of.

The impact of the China-Japan normalization of relations was

---

10 See for example, Nihon kyôsantô chûô iinkai (Japan Communist Party Central Committee) (1975), "Nitchû gokukô kaifuku jitsuken ni saishite" (On the occasion of the implementation of the restoration of relations between Japan and China), September 29, 1972; "Senkaku rettô mondai ni kansuru Nihon Kyôsantô no kenkai" (On the Senkaku islands problem, the Japan Communist Party's point of view), March 31, 1972. *Nihon kyôsantô kokusai mondai jûyô ronbunshû* (Japan Communist Party international issues important collected works), 9.

great. According to a survey conducted by Jiji Press in the 1960s, two to three percent of respondents "liked" China, while thirty to forty percent "disliked" the country.[11] However, according to the Japanese Cabinet Office, the percentage of people who felt friendly toward China increased to an average of 71% during the 1978-88 period.[12] Such a radical turn toward a favorable public opinion on the Peoples Republic of China was clearly the result of the 1972 China-Japan Joint Statement on normalizing relations and the subsequent signing of the Peace and Friendship Treaty between the PRC and Japan in 1978. At this point, one could read a virtuous cycle of the China-Japan non-governmental exchanges during the Cold-War period leading to normalization of state relations between the two countries, which then resulted in the improvement of the Japanese public image of the PRC. However, in the 2000s, Japanese public opinion has taken a radical turn against the PRC. Only about ten percent of the population has a favorable impression of China, and sixty to seventy percent of the respondents felt "hatred."[13] According Jin Xide, a Chinese expert on Japan, the Taiwan and history problems have been "the most important and sensitive issues" between China and Japan, and he calls post-1972 Sino-Japanese relations the "1972 System." What has been confirmed through the system, he states, is that it was "the convergence point" reached from the principles of dealing with the "Taiwan problem, historical consciousness, national security, and territory."[14] What is meant by historical consciousness here, of course, refers to the fact that the 1972 System operated on the basis that while China

11 NHK hôsô seron chôsasho (NHK broadcasting public opinion poll office) (1982), *Zusetsu sengo seronshi* (Diagrammatichistory of postwar polls), Nihon hôsô shuppan kyôkai.

12 Nihon naikakufu (Japan Cabinet Office), "Gaikô ni kansuru seron chôsa" (Public opinion polls on foreign relations). Retrieved March 2, 2012, from http://www8.cao.go.jp/survey/index-gai.html.

13 Ibid.

14 Môri (2006), *Nitchû kankei—sengo kara shinjidai e* (Japan-China relations—from the postwar to a new era), 90.

does not ask for war reparations, Japan has a firm attitude on the Japanese war crimes, at least to the extent that they were identified during the Tokyo War Crimes Tribunal. However, in the 2000s, the Japanese textbook issue, the visits to Yasukuni Shrine, and the Senkaku Island controversy revived the problem of the "historical consciousness," while at the same time "the discourse of the Chinese threat" began to gain traction in Japan. The combination of these two phenomena brought the 1972 System to a crisis point. In the process, the logic of the nation-state, mentioned above, which is linked to the problems of colonialism, rose to the surface. The 1972 System was a system in which China and Japan agreed to "stitch up" the issues of war crimes responsibility with an apology without reparations; in the 2000s this became the source of worsening Sino-Japanese relations. I will now examine the case of the Japan-China Friendship Center, a leading example of the historical conflict "stitched up" with the policy of apology without reparations.

3. The Japan-China Friendship Center and the Japan-China Friendship Movement

1) The Friendship Center and the Confrontation of Communists vs. Communists

From February 28th through March 2nd, 1967, an incident took place at the Good Neighbor Student Center (善隣學生會館)* located at the heart of Tokyo. A violent confrontation broke out between members of the Japan-China Friendship Association, which occupied the lower floors of the five-story building, on the one hand, and Chinese-Japanese students who occupied the top two floors, on the other, and many people were hurt as a

* At the time of this incident, the present-day 'Japan-China Friendship Center' was called the 'Good Neighbor Student Center.' Further details on the history of the Center follow below. In this translation, both 'Student Center' and 'Friendship Center' are used interchangeably, where appropriate -Tr.

result. As for the cause of the physical confrontation, each had their own version. The Friendship Association claimed that their actions constituted lawful self-defense against provocative violence perpetrated by the students. The students claimed that they were the hapless victims of violence initiated by the members of the Association. The truth of the incident has never been fully ascertained. The Student Center and the Japan-China Friendship Association were the two major forces of the Japan-China friendship movement in Japan at the time. What happened between them? The following is the account of the incident in *Shimbun Akahata* (literally 'Newspaper Red Flag' –Tr.), an organ of the Japanese Communist Party:

> For three days, starting from the February 28th, the overseas Chinese students in Japan who are members of the Korakuryo Autonomous Council of Chinese Students in Japan, defectors from the Japan-China Friendship Association, anti-JCP elements who are blind followers of foreign influences, and some overseas Chinese in Japan ganged up and attacked the Japan-China Friendship Association day after day. They beat, kicked, and perpetrated other acts of violence against the Association secretariat staff that formed a scrum in front of the secretariat entrance to fend off these despicable attacks. Many Association members, members of trade unions, and members of democratic organizations from all districts of Tokyo rushed to the scene to lend help, and tens of them—to the extent that we have been able to confirm so far—have sustained injuries that require hospitalization. It betrays common sense that in Tokyo, the capital city of Japan, some foreigners would carry out such violent acts that resulted in bodily injuries in broad daylight.[15]

To such an accusation, the students responded as follows:

> From February 28th to March 2nd, the revisionist Japanese Communist group seized by force part of the Good Neighbor Student Center, turned the false Japan-China Friendship Association into a base camp of anti-China [activities —author], directing rioters every day to madly persecute Chinese-Japanese students who were fighting against the oppression, and Japanese friends who rushed to the scene to aid the students. The group directed the shocking affair of bloodshed, which led to more than twenty casualties, including

15 *Akahata*. March 4, 1967. In *Chûgoku kenkyû* (China research), No. 80. March-April 1977.

> seven who were heavily injured. The madness of the anti-China violence perpetrated by the revisionist Japanese Communist group took place in full view of the Japanese police authorities. The perpetrators have not been arrested, and the safety of the Chinese-Japanese students at the Student Center is still threatened. The situation is grave. The current anti-China bloodshed brought on by the revisionist Japanese Communist group is not an accident. It is part of a grand chorus in which imperialists, revisionists, and reactionaries participate. It is part of the program of anti-China activities systematically and openly planned since last year by the revisionist Japanese Communist group. The current violence is in the same league with the bloody violence of the Soviet revisionists who assaulted Chinese students in the Soviet Union.[16]

The JCP side called the Chinese-Japanese students and their supporters "defectors from the Japan-China Friendship Association and anti-JCP elements who are blind followers of foreign influences" representing only "some of the overseas Chinese living in Japan." The students, on the other hand, called the JCP a "revisionist group" and defined the incident as an "anti-China activity" and denounced what happened as "imperialistic," "revisionist," and "reactionary." The JCP side called the students and their supporters "defectors," by which they meant a "factional political group" that "forced upon Japan [i.e. the JCP –Tr.] the Great Cultural Revolution and the Red Army" of China and who sided with the students by doing so.[17] From the accusations these two groups hurled at each other, one understands more clearly the subtext of the physical clash at the Student Center. The two Communist groups clashed over two divergent lines of communist ideology.

---

16 Kôrakuryô jichikai hakkô (Kôrakyruo self-governing association publishing) (March 1967), "Nikkyô shûseishugi gurûpu no kakyô seinen gakusei ni taisuru shûgeki jiken shinsô" (The truth of the incident of the reactionary JCP group's attack on the overseas Chinese students). Retrieved March 2, 2012, from http://home.a00.itscom.net/konansft/zenrin/sinsou/zenrinsinsou.htm.

17 "Nitchû yûkô kyôkai shûgeki ni kansuru bunkajin sanjûgo shi no kyokô no 'seimei' ni hanron suru" (The rebuttal of the fabricated statement that thirty-five scholars were attacked by the Japan-China Friendship Association), *Nitchû yûkô shimbun*, March 20, 1967. Quoted in *Chûgoku kenkyû* (China research), No. 80, March–April 1977.

In fact, the Student Center incident is a prime example of a Cold-War intra-bloc conflict within the China-Japan friendship movement, or a communist-versus-communist confrontation. At the primary level this confrontation was between the Communist Party in Japan and the Communist Party in China. However, underneath it was the confrontation between the People's Republic of China and the Soviet Union. From the early days of their history, the JCP and the CCP have had friendly relations, and it was in this context of bi-party history that JCP played a central role in the Japan-China friendship movement in Japan. In 1963, in a sign of still-strong friendly relations, the JCP unilaterally expelled pro-Soviet members within its Party in support of the CCP's opposition to the Partial Test Ban Treaty (PTBT). The "trouble" between the CCP and the JCP began on the issues of the Cultural Revolution, but it took the Sino-Russian conflict for that trouble to take a specific form of expression. The JCP-CCP confrontation became explicit after the March 1966 meeting in China between Mao Zedong and Kenji Miyamoto, the Secretary General of the JCP at the time. Their positions on building a united world socialist front in the face of the Vietnam War differed. On the Vietnam issue, China was adamant about taking an anti-U.S. and anti-U.S.S.R line, while the JCP was negative about the anti-Soviet position. Afterwards, the CCP attacked the JCP as "revisionist," and the JCP attacked the CCP as being "hegemonic." Faced with the issue of building a united world front for socialism in the wake of the Vietnam War, the two Communist Parties in Asia each took a different position, and it led to their split. The confrontation between the CCP and JCP continued for over thirty years until the two parties normalized their relations in 1998. Thus, from 1966 onward, the JCP, a former ally of the Japan-China friendship movement in Japan, began intensifying their attacks on the CCP, and it began actively sabotaging the friendship movement.[18]

18 For an example of the JCP's position on the CCP-JCP confrontation, see Kojima (1980),

For example, following its successful inauguration in 1965, the second "China-Japan Youth Friendship Exchange" was scheduled to take place again in 1966 in China with approximately eight-hundred Japanese scheduled to travel to China to participate in the event. However, preparation for the event was thrown into utter disorder when JCP party members or affiliates in the Japan-China Friendship Association and the Council of Japanese Youth Organizations, the two Japanese host organizations, wrecked havoc on organizing the event. In the meantime, the Sato Eisaku government, which was wary of allowing a large group of Japanese to travel to China, took advantage of the internal split in the Japan-China friendship movement and refused to issue passports to the members of the Japanese delegation. The plans for the event eventually fell apart.[19]

The JCP also attempted to sabotage plans to exhibit an anthology of writings by Mao Zedong and other Chinese books at a Chinese economy and trade fair held in Kitakyushu and Nagoya in November and December of 1966, respectively. In the same year the Democratic Youth League of Japan, an affiliate organization of the JCP, refused to participate in the World Conference Against Atomic and Hydrogen Bombs. In November of 1966, the JCP flexed its muscles to encourage the labor union at Asea News Agency[20] to go on strike in an attempt to keep the agency's management under Party influence. Some of the other sabotage acts carried out by the JCP include the closure

---

Nitchû ryôtô kaidan atoshimatsuki (Japan-China inter-party conference settlement.

19 In the previous year, too, the Japanese government refused to issue passports to the members of the Japanese delegation going to China, saying that doing so would be "harmful to Japanese [national -Tr.] security and public order," only to relent after many turns and twists. "Kôpa wo tabi hatate" (Across raging waters). *Nitchû yûkô kyôkai Miyagi-ken renketsusei 50 shûnen kinenshi.* (Japan-China Friendship Association, Miyagi prefecture branch, 50th anniversary publication), 2002.

20 In 1947 it was first established as China News (通訊) Agency. The name was changed to Asea News Agency before being changed back to China News Agency. It distributed news from such Chinese sources as Xinhua News Agency, The People's Daily, and China Central Television (CCTV) to various news outlets in Japan.

of the Kansai office of the Party's Japan-China Travel Agency (1968); the sabotaging of the Educational Review Society's visit to China (1967); the prevention of the screening of *Unity is Powerful*, a documentary film on the first Japan-China Youth Exchange; and the prevention of the showing of *The East Is Red* (東方紅), a historical dramatization of the Chinese Communist revolution. Around this time, the JCP also exerted pressure on bookstores specializing in China, such as the Far East Book Store, Daian Book Store, Uchiyama Book Store, Nauka Book Store, and Saika Book Store, to stop displaying and selling the anthology of writings by Mao and other books.[21]

The discord within the friendship movement in Japan ultimately led to the division of the Japan-China Friendship Association. The association opened the 13th Meeting of the Executive Board on October 25, 1966, but the CCP supporters and the JCP supporters within the Association clashed with each other violently. The point of contention at this meeting was whether or not to adopt the joint statement announced on October 12, 1966 by the Japan-China Friendship Association and its counterpart in China upon the Japanese association's visit to China on the occasion of celebrating the 17th anniversary of the National Day of the People's Republic of China. In the joint statement, what sparked the heated argument was the following evaluation on the Cultural Revolution and the Soviet Union: "The revolutionary actions of the Great Proletariat Cultural Revolution and the Red Guards" are "the most painful blows to U.S. imperialists and reactionaries, and China can never deteriorate into the state of modern revi-

21 Nauka Book Store and Saika Book Store surrendered to this pressure and stopped selling the Mao anthology, while the Far East Book Store opened the new 'Doho (東方) Book Store' in protest. For sabotage acts carried out by JCP, see Nihon chûgoku yûkô kyôkai (seitô) chûô honbuhen (Japan-China Friendship Association (Authentic) central headquarters compilation) (1975), Nitchû yûkô undôshi, (History of the Japan-China friendship movement); *Nitchû yûkô kyôkaihen*, (Japan-China Friendship Association compilation) (2000), *Nitchû yûkô undô gojûnen* (Fifty years of the Japan-China friendship movement).

sionism, at the center of which is the Soviet Union." By a vote of 43 to 13, the supporters of the Cultural Revolution in the Association adopted the joint statement, despite the opposition of its members who were JCP supporters. Afterwards, the pro-Cultural Revolution faction established a separate organization called the Japan-China Friendship Association (Authentic).[22]

By early 1967, the pro-JCP/anti-CCP group of the Japan-China Friendship Association, on the one hand, and the pro-CCP Chinese-Japanese students, on the other, came to cohabitate the Student Center. Thus, what is known as the Good Neighbor Student Center Incident, as I have explained above, was the physical clash between these two forces, and it was not an accident. It was a public manifestation of the battle between pro-JCP and pro-CCP forces vying for hegemony over the social activist movement in Japan at the time. Looking at the incident from this vantage point, one can read it as the beginning of a break in the Socialist bloc ideology that held together and dominated the post-War Japanese socialist movement.

In connection with this point, there is yet another important problematic that one must not miss in the Student Center incident. It is revealed in the following expression used by the JCP as a basis for removing the pro-China faction from the Student Center: "In Tokyo, the capital city of Japan, in broad daylight, some foreigners [have perpetrated -Tr.] such an act of bodily injury." Leaving aside, for the time being, the issue of whether or not Chinese-Japanese should be identified as "foreigners," one can see that, by summoning terms such as "the capital city of Japan" and "some foreigners," the JCP was in fact

22 Nihon chûgoku yûkô kyôkai (seitô) chûô honbuhen (Japan-China Friendship Association (Authentic) central headquarters compilation) (1975), *Nitchû yûkô undôshi* (History of the Japan-China friendship movement). op. cit., "Nihon Chûgoku yûkô daihyôdan to chûgoku nihon yûkô kyôkai daihyôdan to no kyôdô seimei" (Joint declaration of the Japan-China friendship representatives and the China-Japan friendship association representatives) (October 13, 1966), 272.

mobilizing the logic of national sovereignty and Japanese nationality in its rhetoric. This then is the second problematic embedded underneath the surface of the violent Student Center incident. In the background of this intra-bloc, or Communist-versus-Communist, conflict, one finds the operation of the Japanese-versus-foreigner logic, and at the root of this logic one finds the difference between the supporters of the JCP and the Chinese-Japanese students, and their supporters, in regards to who rightfully owns the Center. The pro-JCP Japan-China Friendship Association claimed its right to stay in the building based on a rental contract: "We do not have free access to the second floor meeting hall and the basement storage room which we have rented ourselves and for which we have been paying rent every month. [...] Our association (Japan-China Friendship Association) is a tenant who has a contract with the Good Neighbor Student Center Foundation who has paid required rent. This is protected by civil law and cannot be interfered with by anyone."[23] It continued, "the overseas Chinese students in Japan speak as if the Student Center is their 'property' and cry 'Out!' with the Japan-China Friendship Association, but this is completely preposterous... [The building has been –author] owned, maintained, and managed by the Foundation since the end of the War."[24] Accordingly, they continue, "the overseas Chinese students are not the owners of the Center, rather, the Foundation is."[25] Terao Goro was a JCP member at the time of the Incident and was later expelled from the Party in 1968 and formed the Japanese Communist Party (Left Faction). According to his records, the JCP

23 Ibid., "Nitchû yûkô kyôkai shûgeki ni kansuru bunkajin sanjûgo shi no kyokô no "seimei" ni hanron suru" (The rebuttal of the fabricated statement that thirty-five scholars were attacked by the Japan-China Friendship Association).

24 "Zai nichi kakyô gakusei to taigai mojû bunshira no nitchû yûkô kyôkai shûgeki no shinsô" (The truth of the attack on Japan-China Friendship Association by the resident Chinese students and those blindly following the foreign influences), *Akahata*, March 7, 1967.

25 "Gaikoku seiryoku ni yoru kanshô to bôryoku wa bakasenai" (We will not tolerate foreign forces' intervention and violence), *Nitchû yûkô kyôkai*. March 30, 1967.

accused the Chinese-Japanese students of being "dogmatic," and its members repeatedly employed expressions such as, "Down with foreign interference" and "Down with the Red Guards!" JCP members also repeatedly shouted personally derogatory and ethnically discriminatory remarks directly at the students: "This is Japanese territory! Chinese go back to China!" "*Changkoro* go back!"[26]

In response the Chinese-Japanese students argued that "[f]rom the beginning the Friendship Center has been the property of the People's Republic of China. Because diplomatic relations between China and Japan have not been normalized, the Center is being managed by the Board of the Foundation temporarily on a provisional basis. The Student Center is simultaneously a dormitory for Chinese-Japanese students and a center whose mission is to promote China-Japan friendship and cultural exchanges."[27]

In the view of the Chinese-Japanese students, the rightful owner of the Student Center is the government of the People's Republic of China. However, since no formal ties between China and Japan existed, the Foundation was overseeing the management of the building on behalf of the Chinese government. Furthermore, since the aim of the Student Center was promotion of China-Japan friendship, the anti-CCP/pro-JCP faction of the Japan-China Friendship Association had no right to stay at the Student Center. In contrast, JCP's position was that since the Center facilities belonged to the Foundation, neither the Chinese-Japanese students nor the Chinese government had any ownership right. The central conflict between the two groups (the students and the pro-JCP Friendship Association) was the

26 Terao (1967), *Nitchû fusen no shisô* (Japan-Chinaantiwarthought), See Chapter 1.

27 Kôrakuryô jichikai hakkô (Kôrakyruo self-governing association publishing), "Nikkyô shûseishugi gurûpu no kakyô seinen gakusei ni taisuru shûgeki jiken shinsô" (The truth of the incident of the reactionary JCP group's attack on the overseas Chinese students).

conflict between the JCP and CCP; however it was expressed as a conflict over the ownership of the building. It is noteworthy to observe this fact, because the ownership issue is closely related to Japanese war crimes and post-war Japanese responsibility for them.

2) The Origins of the Conflict Over the Japan-China Friendship Center and the Japan-China Friendship Movement

What is today known as the Japan-China Friendship Center[28] traces its origin to the time before World War II. In 1935, the Association for the Protection and Guidance of Manchukuo Students in Japan established the facilities as the Student Center for Manchukuo Students in Japan. The purpose of the Center was to cultivate pro-Japanese Manchukuo students under the stewardship of the Japanese military (the Greater East Asia Ministry). The costs of the construction and maintenance of the facilities were borne by Manchukuo, but the Center was registered as a Japanese corporation, and a "Manchurian Japanese" was entrusted with the management of the facilities. At one point, a major-general of the Imperial Army presided over Center affairs as its director, and it has had a history of strict control.[29]

On November 10, 1945, the Association for the Protection and Guidance of Manchukuo Students in Japan was disbanded in the wake of the Japanese defeat in World War II and the collapse of Manchukuo. The Chinese foreign students who were unable

28 The history of the Friendship Center name change is itself the history of Sino-Japanese relations. It began as The Center for Manchukuo Students Studying in Japan (June 1935–February 1944). It then became the center for the Association for the Protection and Guidance of Manchukuo Students in Japan (March 1944–1945); Chinese Student Center Dormitory (後楽寮, Korakuryo) (January 1946-?); Good Neighbor Student Center (March 1953–1987); and Japan-China Friendship Center (1987–present).

29 On the Japanese supervision system of Chinese and Manchurian students in Japan, see Kawaji (2003). "Senji taisei shita no zainichi ryûgakusei kyôiku" (The education of exchange students in Japan during wartime), *Intercultural* (2003) 1.

to return to China then changed the name of the building to the "Chinese Student Center" and named the dormitory inside the Center, Korakuryo. During this time the students managed the building. Among the Chinese students who were by this time residents of Japan, those from the mainland mostly stayed in the Chinese Youth Center and the Gandaryo. The students from the former Manchukuo mostly stayed in Korakuryo and Heiwaryo; those from Taiwan stayed mostly in Seiwaryo; and the Taiwanese students from the Koza Naval Arsenal stayed mostly in Seifuryo. Before the end of the War, these room and board facilities were managed by Japan-China Institute (日華學會), the Association for Protection and Guidance of Manchukuo Students in Japan, and the Taiwanese Gakuso (學祖) Foundation, all of which collaborated with Japan in the Japanese invasion of China. However, after the Japanese defeat these organizations were disbanded, and the dormitories were operated autonomously by the resident students.[30]

At the end of the War, the Japanese government saw that the ownership right of these facilities was with the Japanese government, and it began liquidating the assets, including that of the Friendship Center. However, in February 1946, the Civil Property Custodian of the General Headquarters of the Supreme Commander for the Allied Powers (SCAP) in Japan acknowledged that the former Center for Manchukuo Students was an "enemy property" and ordered the Japanese government to stop liquidating the assets. It then commissioned the Japanese government, the Japanese foreign ministry, to manage the property. The SCAP order to suspend the liquidation was a provisional recognition that the ownership right was with China. However, when the People's Republic of China was established in 1949, the American policy to contain China began in earnest. When the Allied occu-

30 Nihon kakyô kajin kenkyûkai (Japan overseas Chinese research group) (2004), *Nihon kakyô, ryûgakusei undôshi* (History of the Japan-resident overseas Chinese exchange student movement), 68-69.

pation government in Japan began its "reverse course" policy on China, its suppression of the Chinese-Japanese students residing at Korakuryo also began in earnest. In the fall of 1951, the Japanese police mobilized 200 armed personnel and raided the Chinese Student Center with a warrant to search for evidences of violations of customs law and violations of the foreigner registration law. In step with the police raid, the media also bombarded the Chinese-Japanese students. The following are various newspaper headlines published around this time: "Raising funds for the Communist Party through smuggling, Red spies engaged in secret maneuvers, Police raid their stronghold, the Chinese Student Center" (Yomiuri Shimbun); "Attacking the secret headquarters of the Chinese Communist smuggling operation. Chinese Student Center searched, Is the ringleader an officer of the Communist China's military?" (Mainichi Shimbun): "Funding from Smuggling by the PRC?" (Asahi Shimbun); "The headquarters of the CCP smuggling operation raided, Funding Japanese Communist Party through drug smuggling?" (Mainichi Shimbun); and "Funding International Communists through smuggling" (Tokyo Shimbun). The media blitz painted the following equation: China= Red=Illegal=Maneuvering behind the Scene=Illegal Drugs. This image was then linked to JCP in an attempt to isolate the Chinese-Japanese students.[31] In this media blitz, the fact that the Chinese-Japanese students' right to stay at Korakuryo was in fact connected with Manchukuo, the puppet state set up by Imperial Japan, recedes into the background.

When the San Francisco Treaty came into force (April 1952) and the Allied occupation of Japan ended, the Japanese government ignored the earlier SCAP order to suspend the liquidation of the Center's assets. It moved to transfer the ownership right to Japanese government. The Japanese foreign ministry thus established the Good Neighbor Student Center Foundation, a

31 Ibid.

not-for-profit corporation, and transferred the assets of the former Manchukuo to the newly incorporated Foundation. The ministry then required the Chinese-Japanese students living at the Center dormitory to sign a rental contract with the new Foundation. In response, the students filed a civil suit seeking a judgment to nullify the establishment of the Foundation, but their action was dismissed on the grounds that the Chinese-Japanese, the party concerned in the case, were disqualified to be a plaintiff. Following this decision, the Foundation demanded that the students move out of the Center on the grounds that the students refused to sign a rental agreement and therefore are "illegally occupying" the Center. The court accepted this argument and judged that the students should be evicted. The students protested against this decision and formed a "Group to Defend Korakuryo" with support from the Chinese-Japanese community and China friendship movement organizations. The students argued that the Center for Manchukuo Students was built with funds from contributions to the Emperor of Manchukuo, and that it therefore was the property of Manchukuo. Now that Manchukuo was abolished and its territory formally transferred to China, it was only right that the Center's ownership belongs to China. Furthermore, this was the basis on which the Allied occupation government ordered the halt of the liquidation of the property earlier. On the other hand, the Japanese foreign ministry argued that the SCAP suspension order became invalid since the San Francisco Treaty came into force. The students pointed out that China neither participated in the Treaty Conference nor signed the Treaty, and that therefore the foreign ministry's basis for nullifying the earlier SCAP order was not valid.[32] In other words, the dispute over the ownership of the Center was related to the nature of Manchukuo and the issues of Japan's war responsibilities. In the wake of these disputes, the students' position was that "while [they] consistently opposed the Japanese govern-

32 Ibid., 192.

ment's claim that the Center is Japanese government property–because the Center actually belongs to China"–they recognized that the "dormitory students are civilians" and they will therefore postpone exercising property rights over the Center "until there is a bilateral decision on the matter between China and Japan upon the normalization of their relations."[33] With this compromise plan on the table, proposed by the students, eighteen Japan-China friendship movement groups began negotiating the plan, and reconciliation was reached in February 1962 through a tripartite meeting that had representatives of the Chinese-Japanese students, the Japanese government, and the Japan-China friendship movement groups.[34] The reconciliation contained the following five points:

> 1) The ownership right of the Center shall remain undecided until there is a normalization of diplomatic relations between Japan and China. 2) It is acknowledged that the Board of the Directors of the Good Neighbor Student Center Foundation has the right to manage the Center. 3) The third and fourth floors of the Center shall be used as a dormitory for Chinese students. 4) The first and second floors of the Center shall be used for the business of promoting Japan-China friendship. 5) Organizations and businesses engaged in activities not related to promoting Japan-China friendship shall be removed from the Center.

According to a decision made at the same meeting, a Chinese-Japanese board member was added to the Foundation's board. Furthermore, a series of Japan-China friendship organizations moved into the building one after another—for example, the Kuraishi Language Institute (1961); the Japan-China Cultural Center (1964); the Japan-China Friendship Association (1965); the Japan-China Academy (1964), and others—and the Center indeed became the center of the Japan-China friendship movement.[35]

---

33 Ibid., 191.

34 Ibid., 186-200.

35 Mitsuoka (March 1967), "Zenrin gakusei kaikan ryûketsu jiken no imi suru mono" (Understanding the Good-Neighbor Student Center bloodshed incident), *Chûgoku kenkyû geppô* (China research monthly).

The compromise plan was in large part the result of the efforts exerted by the Chinese-Japanese students and various Japan-China friendship organizations. However, the compromise was reached also in part because the Japanese foreign ministry had changed its earlier position on the matter, and this change in government position had much to do with the changing political climate of the time. Since the establishment of the People's Republic of China in 1949, and until 1972, exchanges between the PRC and Japan were strictly controlled as each country maintained antagonistic stance toward the other. However, in a limited form, non-political exchanges were taking place actively during the period. In particular, in contrast to the Yoshida administration (1946-47, 1948-54) whose policies were hostile toward China, the Hatoyama Ichiro (1954-56) and Ishibashi Tanzan (1956-57) governments relaxed the earlier administration's hard-line stance. Of course, this flexible stance was in part a response to the full-fledged Chinese peace campaign toward Japan.[36] In 1952, under the policy of "implementing China-Japan activities through people's diplomacy," the Central Committee of

36 In January 1953 Uchiyama Kanzo became the first Japanese citizen to visit the People's Republic of China "legitimately." In June of the same year, a Japanese translation of *People's China* was published. In July of the same year, a Japanese film was shown in PRC for the first time. Since that time bilateral exchanges between the two countries took place actively, albeit in a restricted manner. Some of the high lights of the exchanges include the following: Abe Yoshishige led a delegation of scholars for cultural investigation in China (October 1954); Li Dequan and Liao Chengzhi, leaders of Red Cross Society of China visited Japan (October 1954); a national delegation Japanese scholars visited China via the Soviet Union (June 1955); a delegation of the Japanese Newspaper Association visited the PRC (June 1955); Kabuki actor Ichigawa Enosuke performed in the PRC (October 1955); Kuhara Fusanosuke (1869-1965) a politician, visited China and met with Mao Zedong in the first such meeting for a Japanese (October 1955); Guo Moruo led a delegation of scientists from the Chinese Academy of Sciences in a visit to Japan (December 1955); China participated in the Tokyo Games of the World Table Tennis Championship (April 1956); Mei Lanfang led a troupe of Peking Opera actors to perform in Japan (May 1956); Chinese films were shown during the Japanese "Film Week" (May 1956); a delegation of people representing Chinese literature in Japan visited China (November 1956); and a joint Japan-China film *New Beijing* was produced and publicly shown in Japan (November 1956). From: Shirato (July 1964). "Nitchû bunka kôryû no seika to mondaiten" (Results and problems of Japan-China cultural exchanges), *Ajia keizai junpô*, No. 580.

the CCP established the China-Japan Exchange Office with Liao Chengzhi as its head. In 1954, Zhou Enlai stated that "the people of China distinguish militarists from the people" and "if the peoples of China and Japan continue to pay friendly visits to one another the danger [of the resurrection of militarism—author] can be prevented."[37] In short, it was the Chinese efforts to engage in non-governmental exchanges combined with the Japanese relaxation of hostile policies that people-to-people exchanges flourished in various sectors during this period. For example, the "Japan-China Memorandum on Physical Education" was exchanged (1957). In the same year, the "Joint Statement on Cultural Exchanges Between the Peoples of Japan and China" was also announced. In the economic sector, again, no formal agreements existed between the two governments, but through the LT[38] and MT[39] activities, trade relations continued at the non-governmental level.

In Japan, the forces that led such people-to-people exchanges with China were the leftist groups in Japan. Of the seven leading Japan-China friendship organizations in Japan, three were established after the Japan-China normalization of diplomatic relations. They were the Japan-China Parliamentarian Friendship Federation; the Japan-China Association (1975), which was a special not-for-profit corporation under the jurisdiction of the China affairs department of the Japanese foreign ministry; and the Japan-China Economic Association (1972), a not-for-profit foundation. However, the other four groups, all grassroots organizations, were established during the Cold War era before the

37 Kosuge (2005), *Sengo wakai* (Postwar reconciliation), 185.

38 "LT" here refers to "Memorandum on Japan-China Long-Term Comprehensive Trade" exchanged between Japan and China in 1962. It was a semi-governmental trade agreement in which the government set up a liaison office and guaranteed credits. At the height of its activities, LT trade made up more than 50% of all China-Japan trade.

39 "MT" here refers to the "Japan-China Memorandum Trade," which was signed in 1968. MT replaced LT and was renewable every year. It continued until 1973.

normalization when Japan took a hostile stance toward the PRC. They were the Japanese International Trade Promotion Association, a business organization (1954); the Japan-China Cultural Exchanges Association (1956); the Good Neighbor Student Center (name changed to Japan-China Friendship Center in 1970); and the Japan-China Friendship Association (1950). Of these, the Japan-China Friendship Association and the Good Neighbor Student Center, in particular, allied themselves with the PRC during the Cold War era in demanding that the Japanese government "recognize One China," "abolish the US-Japan Security Treaty," and "compensation to the PRC" as a pre-condition for normalizing the bilateral relations. They were the leading organizations of the Japan-China friendship movement, representing a united front for a coalition of groups. The main coalition groups were the Japanese Communist Party, the Japanese Socialist Party, pro-China elements within the ruling Liberal Democratic Party, and elements of the Japanese New Left. Seen in this context, the 1967 Incident at the Good Neighbor Student Center meant the withdrawal of the Japanese Communist Party, the central force of the united front of the post-war Japan-China friendship movement, from that very movement; the Incident also negated at once of the friendship movement's achievements made over twenty years since 1949.

A change in the political climate of the government administration is also in the background of the clash between the Communists. The Sato Eisaku government, which came to power in November 1964, in particular, was very clear, as was the administration headed by his brother Kishi Nobusuke, about its stance on containing China and giving priority to Taiwan. It pursued the strengthening of Japanese economic cooperation with Taiwan and waged a campaign to stop China from becoming a member of the United Nations.[40] Under these circumstances,

40 Nitchû yûkô kyôkaihen (Japan-China Friendship Association compilation) (2000),

non-governmental exchanges in various sectors suffered setbacks.

As mentioned already, the physical clash at the Student Center between the pro-JCP Japan-China Friendship Association members and the Chinese-Japanese students was an extension of the Chinese-Soviet conflict, the "Second Cold War," filtered through the conflict between the CCP and JCP. On the other hand, it can also be seen an eruption of conflicts latent in the 1962 compromise, which was an example of the issue of Japan's war responsibilities sliding into a fight over the ownership of a building. With this eruption, the confrontational frame changed. Initially, in the first twenty years of the post-war period, the confrontation over the ownership of the Good Neighbor Student Center facilities was between the Japanese government, on the one hand, and Chinese-Japanese and Japan-China friendship organizations writ large, on the other. Since 1967 Incident, this oppositional frame changed to the Japanese government and the JCP versus the Chinese-Japanese and the Japan-China friendship organizations. In other words, if the conflict initially reflected a nation-state (colonial) logic and a Cold-War bloc logic, the new oppositional frame was an amplified structure as the new intra-block oppositional logic combined itself with the old nation-state (colonial) logic.

The conflict over the ownership right of the Friendship Center subsided after the normalization of China-Japan diplomatic relations. However, even after the normalization there was no clear indication of who owned the building. The two governments only succeeded in repeating the 1962 solution of "deferring the ownership right." In 1980, Prime Minister Ohira Masayoshi agreed in a meeting with Chinese Premier Hua Guofeng that the Japan-China Friendship Center should be rebuilt to commemorate the 10th anniversary of the normalization of relations be-

Nitchû yûkô undô gojûnen (Fifty years of the Japan-China friendship movement), 183-186.

tween the two countries. Then, in 1982 China and Japan announced their position on the ownership matter of the Friendship Center. China's position was that it will "defer" its ownership claim, while Japan's position was that it will "not mention the matter." The construction of a new Center began in 1982, and what is today known as the Japan-China Friendship Center in its present form was completed in 1985.[41] The ownership issue still remains unsettled.

4. Concluding Remarks

"Exchange" takes place between units, or between spheres of influences. When an issue is raised about an exchange, it is to raise an issue about a barrier that restricts the movement between units/spheres. For a sphere or a unit to be a sphere or a unit, there has to be a wall that demarcates it as such, and it has to be possible to differentiate what is inside and outside of this wall. It does not matter how low the wall may shrink, or how insignificant the distinction between the inside and outside of the wall can become; as long as the exchange presupposes the existence of a nation-state, the walls do not by themselves generate a dynamic force to cancel the nation itself. Accordingly, 'exchange'/'anti-exchange' is simply another name for the sovereignty of a nation-state. However, when the logic

41 In October 1982, the Chinese government made the following seven-point proposal: 1) If the goal of the new Center satisfies the goal of promoting Japan-China friendship, [China] defers property claims over the Center; 2) The rights and interests of prior tenants shall be protected; 3) In the new board, Chinese-Japanese director(s) shall constitute a certain percentage; 4) The new board shall include a representative from China; 5) Construction plans for the new building and the selection of new board members shall be prepared by the existing board directors. However, at an appropriate time they should obtain the approval of both the Chinese and Japanese governments; 6) The property lot and the building shall not be sold; and 7) China shall bear the construction cost of 500 million yen.
Kawamoto (August 1983), "Chûgoku shinryaku, tekishi, besshi no shôchô 'zenrin gakusei kaikan" (A symbol of Chinese aggression, hostility, and contempt, the 'Good Neighbor Student Center'), *Ajia keizai junpô* (1268), 14-16.

of the Cold War is superimposed upon the logic of a nation-state, the problem becomes much more complicated. That is to say, when the logic of a nation-state is combined with the logic of the Cold War, the wall operates in a much more obstructive way. The Cold-War regime that dominated post-war international relations, in particular, brought about the condition in which international relations cannot be explained simply with the logic of national sovereignty. Accordingly, exchange/anti-exchange is based simultaneously on the logic of national sovereignty and at the same time on the logic of the Cold War. Of course, the two are not neatly separable, nor do they always necessarily contradict or comply with each other. That is the nature of such a wall; its reality is layered. For example, let us assume exchanges take place through people, goods, money, and information. The wall that obstructs their exchange (flow) usually appears in the form of a territorial border between countries. Even if the logic of the Cold War is used to either lower or raise the wall, it is still expressed and activated through the unit of a nation-state. In this sense, any discussion of exchange is a discussion of a nation state. However, the ideology of exchange/anti-exchange cannot always be explained with the logic of a nation-state. That is because in the case of multiple nation-states forming an alliance, and when the alliance is pitted against another such alliance, there has to be a common logic that penetrates across all nations within each alliance. In other words, there has to be a transnational ideology. If we call this transnational ideology a bloc logic, what determines an international exchange and anti-exchange is the logic of a nation-state and at the same time the transnational bloc ideology. This is why one must look at a state of confrontation between countries from the layered perspective of both a nation-state and bloc. If one applies this layered perspective on China-Japan relations in the context of the Student Center incident, it becomes clear that the transnational logic, that is, the Cold War logic, is the main culprit that produced an "absence" of official exchanges between China and Japan. In the absence of bi-national official exchange, the problem of the Friendship Center could not find an official solution, and it could not but be kept inside the nation-state system of Japan. At the same time, however, one cannot say that the dispute over the Friendship Center was caused solely by the Cold War logic, because the Japanese government's attitude toward the ownership issue of the Friendship Center is connected to how it sees Japan's wars of aggression. When the Allied occupation government made the liquidation suspension decision, mentioned earlier, it is probably because the Americans felt that it was consistent with the kind of Cold War regime they were trying to build. Accordingly, the Japanese government's claim to the ownership of the Student Center property is linked to its attitude of denying responsibility for its war of invasion and of denying the illegitimacy of owning property acquired through such a war. In this sense, the Japanese government's attitude on the Student Center problem was based on a nation-state logic combined with the logic of imperialism.

Secondly, there is the issue of who is the subject (agent) in bi-national exchanges. Theoretically, in the absence of official governmental exchanges, any exchange that takes place between the two countries could not but emerge out of the desires of the citizens independent of the state. In such a case, civil society and the government at times clash with, and at other times complement each other. However, unless the people involved are a political group aiming at overthrowing its own government, the goal of their engagement in bi-national exchanges is ultimately to act as a "point man" who points to official bilateral exchanges. Thus, in the absence of intergovernmental exchanges, the exchange agent cannot but be the people; but when intergovernmental exchanges are activated, the role of the people either becomes secondary or changes completely, even thought they had earlier played the leading role in initiating the intergovernmental exchanges. From the time when the People's Republic was established in 1949 until 1972, both countries defined each other as a "potential enemy." It was the period of the absence of official exchanges. Mori Kazuko, a sinologist based in Japan, has called this period of mutual animosity "the middle of the Cold War," indicating that China-Japan relations were restricted by the East-West Cold War logic, Japan-US relations, and Japan-Taiwan relations.[42] Iwamura Michio, formerly a journalist, who played a crucial role in establishing the Japan-China Friendship Association, denies the notion that the Japan-China normalization of relations was a result of the Japanese government's and business sector's efforts to develop a new market in China; instead, he argues that the normalization was the result of "changing times" and the efforts of the people.[43] However, as mentioned already, it cannot be said that the China-Japan normalization of diplomatic relations was built upon the succession of the achievements of post-war Japan-China non-governmental exchanges prior to 1972. Accordingly, the role of civil society in this cannot but be very limited.

This leads to the third problem. The "people" as in the "people-to-people" exchanges, or the exchange agents who are independent of the government, were by no means homogeneous. The agents of exchanges participating in the Japan-China friendship movement by and large had various political inclinations. Needless to say, the Japanese Communist Party played the central role. For as long as the JCP advocated proletarian internationalism, its connection to the CCP was only natural. However, as mentioned earlier, the intra-bloc conflict between the PRC and the Soviet Union during the Cold War era, a major international conflict, brought about a lasting fissure in the JCP-CCP alliance. Furthermore, since the JCP's change of direction in 1955, in which it adopted parliamentarian democracy as part of its agenda and settled itself within the boundary of a nation-state, it was impossible for it to continue to maintain proletarian internationalism

42 Môri (2006), op. cit., see Chapter 1.

43 Iwamura (1973), "Nitchû yûkô no shin dankai" (A new phase in Japan-China friendship). *Chûgoku kenkyû geppô* (China research monthly), 300-301.

that went beyond the boundary of the nation. Thus, the Japanese Communist Party took "refuge" inside the national border of Japan in the name of "autonomy" when it faced a change, an intra-bloc conflict, inside the Cold War regime. At least since 1955, the Party had armed itself with the logic of a nation-state. The end result of the JCP taking this "refuge" was the Student Center incident, and it meant that on the issue of the war responsibility the Japanese Communist Party took sides with the Japanese government.

Bibliography

Hara Yoshihisa (2000), *Sengoshi no naka no Nihon Shakaitô* (The Japan Socialist Party in postwar history), Chûô Kôron Shinsha.

Iwamura Michio (February 1973), "Nitchû yûkô no shin dankai" (A new phase in Japan-China friendship), Chûgoku kenkyûsho (China research institute), *Chûgoku kenkyû geppô* (China research monthly), 300-301.

Kawaji Yuka (2003), "Senji taisei shita no zainichi ryûgakusei kyôiku" (The education of exchange students in Japan during wartime), *Intercultural*, 1, Nihon kokusai bunka gakkai.

Kawamoto Toshio, August (1983), "Chûgoku shinryaku, tekishi, besshi no shôchô 'zenrin gakusei kaikan'" (A symbol of Chinese aggression, hostility, and contempt, the 'Good-Neighbor Student Center'), *Ajia keizai junpô* (1268).

Kojima Masaru (1980), *Nitchû ryôtô kaidan atoshimatsuki* (Japan-China inter-party conference settlement), Shin Nippon Shuppansha.

Kosuge Nobuko (2005), *Sengo wakai* (Postwar reconciliation), Chûkô Shinsho.

Mitsuoka Gen (March 1967), "Zenrin gakusei kaikan ryûketsu jiken no imi suru mono" (Understanding the Good Neighbor Student Center bloodshed incident), *Chûgoku kenkyû geppô* (China research monthly), Chûgoku kenkyûsho (China research institute).

Môri Kazuko (2006), *Nitchû kankei—sengo kara shinjidai e* (Japan-China relations—from the postwar to a new era), Iwanami shoten.

Nagata Yôko (1990), *Zoku jûroku no bohyô* (The sixteen gravestones), Sairyûsha.

NHK hôsô seron chôsasho (NHK broadcasting public opinion poll office) (1982), *Zusetsu sengo seronshi* (Diagrammatic history of postwar polls), Nihon hôsô shuppan kyôkai.

Nihon chûgoku yûkô kyôkai (seitô) chûô honbuhen (Japan-China Friendship Association (Authentic) central headquarters compilation) (1975), *Nitchû yûkô undôshi* (History of the Japan-China friendship movement), Seinen Shuppansha.

Nihon kakyô kajin Kenkyûkai (Japan overseas Chinese research group) (2004), *Nihon kakyô, ryûgakusei undôshi* (History of the Japan-resident overseas Chinese exchange student movement), Nihon kakyô pô, 68-69.

Nihon kyôsantô chûô iinkai (Japan Communist Party Central Committee) (1975), *Nihon kyôsantô kokusai mondai jûyô ronbunshû (Japan Communist Party international issues important collected works)* (9), Nihon kyôsantô chûô iinkai shuppankyoku.

Nitchû yûkô kyôkaihen (Japan-China Friendship Association compilation) (2000), *Nitchû yûkô undô gojûnen* (Fifty years of the Japan-China friendship movement), Tôhô Shoten.

Sakaguchi Hiroshi (1993), *Asama sansô 1972* (Part two), Sairyûsha.

Shirato Norio (July 1964), "Nitchû bunka kôryû no seika to mondaiten" (Results and problems of Japan-China cultural exchanges), *Ajia keizai junpô*, 580.

Takeuchi Yoshimi (1966), *Nihon to Ajia* (Japan and Asia), Chikuma Shobô.

Takeuchi Yoshimi (1980–82), *Takeuchi Yoshimi zenshû* (Collected works of Takeuchi Yoshimi), Vol. 11, Chikuma Shobô.

Terao Gorô (1967), *Nitchû fusen no shisô* (Japan-China antiwar thought), Atôsha.

Yamadaira Shigeki (2011), *Rengô sekigun monogatari, kôen* (The story of the United Red Army, red flame), Tokuma Shoten.

"Repatriates" in Movement:
Zainichi Koreans Moving to South Korea in a "Post-Cold War" Era and Re-composition of Border

by CHO Kyung-hee

Humanities Korea Research Professor
Institute for East Asian Studies at SungKongHoe University

1. Return/Migration of Diaspora

The high tide of globalization in the "post-Cold War" era has drawn much scholarly attention and interest, and as a result modern and contemporary society has been re-interpreted from the perspective of mobility. East Asia, in particular, has drawn much attention in this discussion as a region with one of the most dynamic human and capital flows in the world. In the historical background of this phenomenon, one can easily find the presence of the Koreans who experienced dispersion under the Japanese colonial rule in the early 20th century, and under the Cold War regime following the national liberation in 1945. Immigration occurs in close connection with colonial rule. In the case of Zainichi Koreans[1], or Koreans who mostly migrated and

1 In this chapter "Zainichi Koreans" or "Zainichi," in short, are used interchangeably

settled in Japan during the colonial period, their experience continued to be shaped by colonialism even after the national liberation; furthermore, the division of the Korean peninsula into North and South Koreas, also the result of colonialism, profoundly intervened in their everyday life. As a result, Zainichi Koreans have long been perceived in South Korea either as a potential espionage and security threat, or as a source of economic aid to the nation.

However, democratization in Korea, surging globalization, and the historical events of North-South Korean reconciliation in the early 2000s accelerated the traffic of Zainichi "*dongpo*" (compatriot(s)) visiting South Korea; this brought an opportunity for many Zainichi Koreans to re-define their relationship with "fatherland." Today, because of their cultural plurality and border identity, they can play the role of a mediator between their country of residence and "fatherland." If the experiences of Koreans migrating to Japan reflected the reality of colonialism and Cold War in modern Korean history, the recent phenomena of Zainichi Koreans' return/migration to Korea reflect post-Colonial and post-Cold War challenges. Are the returning Zainichi "repatriates" or "migrants"? Are they "one of us (*dongpo*)" or "the other (*taja*)"? Is this dichotomy valid from a diaspora perspective? This chapter will focus on the experience of Zainichi Koreans moving to Korea mostly after 2000, the "post-Cold War era," and examine the boundary lines they face and the border politics involved.[2]

---

to refer to people from Joseon, or the Korean peninsula, who migrated to Japan during Japan's occupation of Joseon, regardless of their current nationality or particular organizational affiliation.

2 My use of the term "post-Cold War" in this chapter is informed not only by the collapse of the international regime of Cold War in the 1990s, but also by the efforts to reconcile North-South hostilities on the Korean peninsula after 2000, in particular, and by the changes those efforts effected. Thus "post-Cold War" here refers to an orientation, not a reality. As I explain in this chapter, the Cold-War regime of the North-South Korean division (the Division system) still continues. This reality, and the recent aggravation of North-South Korean tension, is a testament to the self-contradiction in the periodization of "Cold-War" and "post-Cold War" era.

In migrating to and settling in South Korea, Zainichi Koreans face not only physical borderlines but a complex set of them. *Joseon*, *Hanguk* (South Korea), and *Ilbon* (Japan) are the boundaries of nationality and language that institutionally and culturally determine whether or not a Zainichi is a "*Hangugin* (South Korean)." Also, anything relating to the General Association of Korean Residents in Japan, or Chongryon, is subject to ideological censorship, and the Zainichi are made deeply aware of it. These boundaries are historical traces imposed upon them from without; at the same time, these are the important boundary lines Zainichi themselves use to construct their own identities and differences. Ordinarily, Zainichi Koreans migrating to South Korea deal with the nation's institutions and the ideologies of boundary either by compromising with or avoiding them, or by confronting or making the most of them. The purpose of this chapter is to examine border politics taking place in this mutualnegotiation process and thereby delineate the salient aspects of how the relationships are defined between the Zainichi diaspora and "fatherland."

Recently, studies on the return/migration of Zainichi Koreans have started to appear.[3] These studies have focused their attention on the Zainichi's cross-border decision and on the revelation of their identities made in the context of the broadening contact between Zainichi and South Korean society. They are excellent sources for learning about the post-Cold War era migration ex-

3 KWON Suk-in studied younger-generation Zainichi Koreans in South Korea and examined how they—who chose to "repatriate" in order to become "a more complete Korean—reworked or compromised their notion of their own ethnic identity as they faced lack of public understanding in Korean society (KWON, 2008). HAN Yeong-hae studied third-generation Zainichi Koreans who have changed their "Joseonjeok" status and became South Korean citizens. She focused on their choice in the context of their family and social relationships (HAN, 2011). Also, from the perspective of cultural capital, KIM Ye-rim focuses on Zainichi Koreans' cultural practices in Korea and examines the complex relationship between the state institutions that in really still constrain the young generation, on the one hand, and the desire of the subject, on the other (KIM, 2009).

periences of Zainichi Koreans and about how they negotiate with Korean society. However, these studies do not account for the political changes that have taken place in South Korea more recently, which have resulted in restricting the mobility of Zainichi Koreans. Building upon these prior studies, this chapter will also highlight the condition of Zainichi Koreans whose mobility has been put under restraint recently. The purpose is to thereby shed light on the intersection where post-Cold War and Cold-War realities cross each other in this "era of post-Cold War."

It should be noted that the spread of the notion of 'diaspora' based on the notion of mobility often misses the dualistic prescription for Zainichi Korean mobility. Since the publication of *The Diaspora' Diaspora* (Brubaker, 2005), questions on the inflation of the notion of 'diaspora' have been raised in earnest. The classic concept of the Diaspora specializes in the historical experience of Jews, in which an exclusive marriage of a certain territory with a certain culture is designated as "the origin" where all Diaspora must return too. This essentialist concept of Diaspora has long lost its power of persuasion, and it has been replaced by the notion of symbolic diaspora, which takes into account the on-going phenomena of post-colonization, the movements and displacements taking place in the globalization process, and cultural hybridization (Hall, 1993; Clifford, 1997). In Korea, too, since the introduction of the notion of "diaspora" in the 2000s, its discourse has privileged the notions of diversity and difference and dispersibility vis-à-vis the notions of exclusivity and centrality inherent in the *minjok* (nation/ethnic) or *dongpo* ('compatriot') paradigm.

What I propose is that one must be careful about one's discovery of diaspora mobility and dispersibility, and of the deterritorialized identity, as one may fail to overlook the reality of the non-mobility a diaspora. 'Non-mobility' here refers to forced locality, not a phenomenon that is part of the generalized local-ization process accompanied by globalization; in other words, it refers to a predisposition to settle, or the difficulty of being able to move again, as a result of the experience of a separation. On this subject, Sonia Ryang has said that the dynamic and static aspects should be distinguished in the concept and conditions of diaspora (Ryang, 2002). In other words, those who do not move, or those who cannot but be confined to where they are, regardless of their intention, constitute a large part of those who are characterized as diaspora. The reality of Zainichi Koreans today demand that we examine its dynamism in light of the prescriptions of both post-Cold War and Cold War, or in light of both their mobility and immobility. In this chapter, attention will be focused, in particular, on how Zainichi Koreans address the dynamics of mutually-opposing forces that define who they are as they try to define their relationship with Korean society; this chapter also examines the strategic choices they make in the process.

Methodologically, this chapter tries to reconstruct, through interviews and observation of second-and third-generation Zainichi Koreans, their experience of moving to South Korea and their every-day border-consciousness and negotiation process. Interviews were conducted between June and August of 2011, mostly in Japanese. Eleven (11) interviewees were selected among second-and third-generation Zainichi who currently live in Korea or have lived in Korea in the past; additionally four (4) more interviewees were selected among Zainichi Koreans who live in Japan who are currently having difficulty moving to Korea. In terms of the legal status of the interviewees, three (3) are "Joseonjeok;" one (1) is a "Korean with a foreign nationality (*oeguk gukjeok dongpo*)," or a Japanese national; and the rest of them (11) are "Korean nationals living abroad (*jaeoe gukmin*)" who maintained their permanent resident status in Japan. Of the total fifteen interviewees, eight had the experience of attending Korean Schools in Japan. Of the seven interviewees who attended only

Japanese schools, three had the experience of having worked in a *minjok* (ethnic Korean) organization when they were in college, meaning that most of the interviewees had a certain level of ethnic Korean community network and ethnic cultural capital. Also, except for three, all interviewees had Masters or higher academic degrees. Of the fifteen interviewees, nine either worked at a college or language *hagwon* for Japanese, or was attending a graduate school. The high educational level and the concentration of their careers in academic or otherwise educational field were a distinctive characteristic of the interviewee population.

The first reason for this skewed population is the snowball sampling method I used in which interviewees are introduced to the researcher by friends and acquaintances. Secondly, it can be the result of excluding short-term visitors, or those who come to Korea to learn language or as a foreign student.[4] It was often the case that the interviewees—who were introduced to this researcher by her friends and their friends—already knew each other through their involvement in the post-2000 Korea-Japan joint academic or NGO activities, or through their involvement in ethnic Korean community organizations in Japan. Ultimately, the composition of this sample population was good in that I was able to highlight the network of Zainichi Koreans who were redefining their relationship with South Korea as they shared among themselves the contemporary conditions.

Of course this human network is neither completely transparent nor stable. In coming to South Korea they made transborder decisions with non-Divisional identity; but the complexity of their choices and identities carries with it the instability of being easily exposed to border ideology that Korean society still

4 The exclusion of short-term visitors was intentional on my part. In representing Zainichi Koreans moving to South Korea, I wanted to focus on their negotiation strategies, rather than on the discriminations and the hurt the Zainichi commonly experience in Korea.

activates. This chapter is an attempt to bring up to date the current dynamics between Korean society and Zainichi Koreans as post-Cold War subjects traverse through and negotiate with Cold War structure.

2. Nationality on the border

A nation-state comes into existence by drawing lines that divide territories and people, and as such its borders are intrinsically artificial. Historically, we have gone through imperialism and Cold War, and we have come to accept the sovereignty of a nation-state, defined by its borderlines, as the universal and immutable principle. Regardless of what political violence they are a product of—a war, an occupation, or a colonial rule, for example—national borders and national identity of an individual are constantly justified in every-day life, and thus they are perceived as part of nature. That mobility has become an issue in an era of globalization is an indication of the extent to which territories and humans have been demarcated along national borders and nationalities. On the Korean peninsula, the artificial division of North and South Korea has brought separation of families, division of the sphere of economic activities, and suspension of communication. However, when the North-South demarcation line is taken for granted as natural national borders, the nationality issue surrounding Zainichi Koreans becomes a labyrinth from which no exit can be found. Nationality determines one's belongingness, but for people who live on the edges of its border, its truth is not self-evident but always insecure and fluid.

The legal status of Zainichi Koreans in Japan has its origin in post-war Japan's Alien Registration system. In government records, "Joseon" was a statistical mark that Japanese officials used to unilaterally refer to all Koreans still remaining in Japan after the end of World War II. In fact, "Joseon" was not so much a sign of nationality as it was a sign of locality. Since then, to this day, a certain number of people have kept, for many reasons, their status as marked in the Japanese government record, without acquiring South Korean citizenship; they are called "Joseonjeok."[5] A characteristic feature of the post-Cold War era in Korea is the rapid increase of former students of Korean schools in Japan, who are known as "Chongryon-affiliated Koreans," moving to South Korea. Many of them had maintained their Joseonjeok status until they decided to come to South Korea, only changing the status and obtaining South Korean citizenship in order to enter South Korea. From the very first stage of their attempt to enter South Korea, they face the reality of the North-South Korea "Division system." Some give up entry into South Korea, others give up their Joseonjeok status as instructed by the Korean Consulate in Japan. In other words the Joseonjeok Zainichi in Japan must go through the process of acquiring South Korean citizenship in order to enter South Korea at all. If the passport identification system is characterized by "monopoly over the legitimate means of movement" (Torpey, 2000), passport issuance by a divided nation signifies, in itself, a regime competition and a state power at work that is at the root of all nation-making. Furthermore, the fact that the South Korean Consulate in Japan colludes with the Japanese Alien Registration system to nationalize Zainichi Koreans as South Korean citizens even smacks of the historical collaboration of Koreans with Japanese under the colonial rule.

After the 1990s, South Korean government made a way for Joseonjeok Zainichi Koreans to enter South Korea on a tempo-

---

5 According international law, each nation defines its own nationality according to its nationality law. "Joseonjeok" (literally "of Joseon" -Tr.) is a Japanese designation, and it does not refer to the citizens of *Choson Minjujuui Inmin Konghwaguk*, or the Democratic People's Republic of Korea (DPRK). Moreover, Japan does not have a formal diplomatic relations with North Korea (DPRK), and North Korean citizenship is not officially recognized in Japan. However, the South Korean government has considered Joseonjeok Zainichi as *de facto* North Korean nationals on the grounds that they have refused to take South Korean nationality, and the government has routinely been asking them to formally take on South Korean citizenship.

rary-stay basis by issuing "travel certificates."[6] This had limitations, but it did provide a way—the only way—for Joseonjeok Zainichi Koreans to keep their historical identity and still visit South Korea. However, since the current administration took office, in 2008, the number of rejection of the travel certificate applications by Joseonjeok has increased dramatically, and since the sinking of a South Korean Navy ship the *Cheonan*, all application by Joseonjeok for a travel certificate have been rejected. In Japan, the number of Zainichi Koreans who send their children to a Korean school, or who maintain the Joseonjeok status has been decreasing annually. Today, Joseonjeok Zainichi are a minority group, and they constitute less than ten percent of all Zainichi Koreans in Japan.[7] In other words, what this points to is a reality in which one has to move nationality in order secure mobility to South Korea.

In this regard, the Joseonjeok issue is not an issue that only concerns the status of the few remaining Joseonjeok; it is an on-going problem that illustrates the historical and contemporaneous status of Zainichi Koreans, which has always been largely determined by colonial powers and then by the forces of the Cold War politics and the North-South division on the Korean peninsula. In other words, the congenital instability surrounding the nationality status of Zainichi Koreans is the compendium

6 Article 10 (Guarantee of Entry into Korea of ethnic Koreans Living Abroad) of the South-North Korea Exchange and Cooperation Law legislated in 1990 stipulates that "When an ethnic Korean living abroad, who neither is a foreign national nor possesses a passport issued by the Republic of Korea, wishes to visit South Korea, he or she must possess a Travel Certificate issued in accordance with the Passport Law, Article 14, Paragraph 1." This article became the basis for issuing the travel certificates to Joseonjeok Zainichi Koreans.

7 According to the foreign nationals statistics announced by Japanese Ministry of Justice, of the total 2,134,151 aliens registered in Japan, South Korean nationals/Joseonjeok account for 565,989 (Of this number, 395,234 are "special-status permanent residents" and 8,374 are "settlers"). No separate figures are available for the South Korean nationals and Joseonjeok, so an exact figure for Joseonjeok is not known. However, it is estimated that there are now approximately 50,000 of them. The total number of Zainichi Koreans who acquired Japanese citizenship from 1952 to 2010 is 326,671.

of a delayed post-colonial and post-Cold War reality. Of the eleven interviewees who had South Korean citizenship, seven of them had acquired it as a child, or otherwise as part of growing up in their family. The other four interviewees who were Korean nationals gave up their "Joseonjeok" status specifically so that they could come to South Korea. One such interviewee, Choe Jun-hyeong[#] (Male, 33), who acquired South Korean citizenship in 2006, still remembers vividly the fear he had experienced when he was traveling on a North Korean passport and passing through the Incheon Airport on his travel abroad as a college student. He went to a Japanese school, but he grew up hearing from his parents about "Joseon" before the country was divided, and what it meant. As a student, he had opportunities to come in contact with Zainichi communities and the One Korea Unification Festivals held in the Osaka area. He had even worked as a volunteer staff member for the event. However, there were limitations, and he felt that there was not much about himself that he could claim as Zainichi. Around that time, he participated in an NGO workshop on East Asia solidarity and met many Koreans who became important in his life. It then became a natural choice for him to change the nationality and to come to Korea. He had fears about the process, but once he tried it was not at all difficult. He feels that historical significance of having to maintain a "Joseonjeok" status is vanishing.

The institutional stability and the freedom of movement that South Korean nationality allows do not necessarily translate immediately into a stability of personal identity and freedom for Joseonjeok Zainichi Korean. The gap between the historical significance and the functional significance of the nationality is not resolved by securing mobility. Even after acquiring a South Korean passport, one suffers from an undefined sense of "guilt" toward the Zainichi community in Japan and "alienation." In the

---

Names of the interviewees are pseudonyms.

case of KANG Tae-hwan (Male, 32), who had acquired South Korean citizenship most recently among the interviewees, he was staying in Korea on a long-term basis on his "Joseonjeok" status when the battleship *Cheonan* incident occurred. He applied for a routine renewal of his travel certificate, and it was denied. He had works to do in Korea, and he had to apply for a South Korean passport in a hurry against his own wish. He had maintained close relationship with the Korean school community in Japan, and while the South Korean Consulate in Japan was pressuring him to change his status, there was also a tacit community pressure from Japan to not take it up. The responses of the Koreans around him in Korea were various. Some consoled him and said they were sorry, others congratulated and welcomed him. Kang's case illustrates how the uncertain identity of "Joseonjeok" can be deployed, in certain crisis situations, as a stage on which discursive and political supremacy is fought out by two opposing Cold War forces. As KIM Ye-rim has pointed out, the acquisition of South Korean citizenship by a Joseonjeok Zainichi reveals the paradox and tension in which the post-Cold War opportunities for mobility serve as a venue for exercising the Cold-War ideology of nation (KIM, 2009: 368).

As late as the 1990s, Zainichi Koreans often distanced themselves from certain Zainichi organizations or community activities if they had plans to have dealings with South Korea. Considering that, the situation now is very different. The interviewees who have obtained South Korean citizenship since 2000 have done so, using nationality as a means of movement after meeting people in South Korea who became special to them. A move to South Korea brings practical benefits to them. It brings them a new routine in life and an expansion of human network. However, the acquisition of the citizenship, for them, is a rational choice, on the one hand, and a compromise, on the other hand. The institutional crossing of the border, from being a "Joseonjeok" to being a South Korean national, does not so much "re-set" their lives as it activates more microscopic border politics in continuing their lives. The conflict that arises between the historical and symbolic significance and the functional value attached to one's nationality status is not easily resolved in their relationship with either Korean society or various Zainichi communities. The conflict and a sense of responsibility that they experience is a testimony that for Zainichi Koreans choosing a nationality does not constitute freedom of choice.

3. "Dangerous Nationals"

As we examined above, the Zainichi acquisition of South Korean nationality takes on a certain form of a nationalization drive that is dictated by post-Cold War conditions and the globalization phenomena of the era. What is ironic, then, is that the South Korean government that is behind the nationalization drive is turning the South Korean nationals of Zainichi origin into problematic citizens, again. One of the major institutional changes that has taken place recently regarding the rights of Korean nationals living abroad is that they now have the right to vote. In 2009, the public offices election law was revised in Korea, and starting with the National Assembly election in April 2012, which is followed by the presidential election in December of the same year, Korean nationals living overseas can now cast ballots in South Korean elections. However, according to the government, the extension of political rights based on nationality is seriously compromising security of the nation given the condition of the North-South confrontation. Within some political circles, the Ministry of Diplomacy and Commerce, Mindan (the Korean Residents Union in Japan), and Korean Consulate in Japan, the question of how to categorize Chongryon-affiliated Zainichi with South Korean citizenship has become a major concern.

For example, in its New Year's message in 2011, Mindan declared: [We] have identified that there are many compatriots (*dongpo*) who have acquired the right to vote in Korean elections by changing their status from Joseonjeok to Hangukjeok (of Republic of Korea) and by acquiring a South Korean passport, but are still serving in Chongryon activities." They have thus taken it to be their organizational task in 2012 to respond to the "2012 Problem" by "strictly distinguishing them from those who have a complete break with Chongryon."[8] More recently, there has also been a move among political circles in South Korea to prevent "Chongryon ballots" in the elections, criticizing the South Korean government as the "government that gives suffrage to North Korea and Chongryon." A government official stated that "spies who enter the country disguised as Korean nationals living abroad pose not only security threats but can also influence elections next year." This official added that since the number of such espionage agents entering Korea is "expected to rise sharply with the general election coming next year, [the government plans to] not permit acquisition of citizenship by any overseas Koreans suspected of having North Korean ties and reinforce monitoring of major suspects even after they acquire [South Korean] citizenship."[9] Thus the government is attempting to put the blame for the loophole in the government's decades-old nationalization project on the "impure" identity of overseas Koreans. Thus the problem is no longer the Zainichi Koreans who maintain their "Joseonjeok" status, but the countless "former Joseonjeok" who are now South Korean nationals. These nationals are now more dangerous than ever, because their impurity is no longer institutionally visible.

Such Cold War mentality on the part of the Korean government, and the "ideology check campaign" being carried out by

8 [Haeseol (Opinion)] "2012 (i-cheon sibi)nyeon munje'ran jongbuk seryeok-ui chaek-dong bongsoehaeya' (The '2012 Problem' of Having to Seal Off Maneuvers by Pro-North Korean Forces)."Mindan shinmun, December 27, 2010. http://bit.ly/kWHMRK.

9 "'Gamyeon' sseun bulsun seryeok... naenyeon yangdae seongeo bburichae dwiheundeul uryeo (Impure Elements behind a 'Mask'... A Cause for Concern about Uprooting the Major Elections Next Year)." *Munhwa Ilbo*, October 20, 2011.

the Korean Consulate in Japan, are in fact causing concrete difficulties and new forms of pain in the lives of Zainichi Koreans in Japan. Li Gyeong-hwa (Female 25) is a naturalized South Korean citizen, but she was refused a South Korean passport by the Korean government because she had visited North Korea in the past as part of her group activity. She received a call from the Korean Consulate in Japan and was told that "It is illegal for a Korean national to engage in Chongryon activities, and a visit to North Korea without permission from South Korean government is a crime." After the phone call, she could not join her family on a family trip. What the Consulate officer told her, that "your ideas are still Joseonjeok," greatly shocked her. Over eighty percent of Zainichi Koreans today are estimated to have South Korean nationality. The "ideology check" by South Korean government has brought about the result of a constant and mutual distrust among Zainichi Koreans, and between South Korean community and the Zainichi, of which there are now many examples. Apart from that, the Korean Consulate in Japan has been rolling out various restriction measures. For example, after conducting a background check on individual Zainichi Koreans with South Korean nationality, the Consulate would arbitrarily reduce individual passport valid period or refuse to renew the passport all together.[10] Having experienced such restrictions first hand, many of them have said that they will simply not vote. They do not want to exercise a right that draws new lines of exclusion.

10 On September 20, 2010, a "partially revised" Enforcement Decree of the Passport Act was promulgated. The revised Decree had a new clause in Part 2, Article 6 (Passport Expiration), Paragraph 5: "A member of an anti-state organization as defined by National Security Act Article 2 who resides abroad, who can potentially cause great damages on national security, maintenance of [social] order, and reunification and diplomatic polices: A period within the range of one to five years, as determined by the Minster of Foreign Affairs and Trade, according to the degree of the danger perceived." It further stipulates that, whether or not this clause applies to a particular person [applying for a passport renewal] shall be determined in consultation with relevant administrative agency.

While anti-communism has lost its former fierceness in South Korea, it is still the official ideology, and the recent aggravation of North-South Korean tension justifies its existence. The election year campaigns targeting Zainichi Koreans mentioned above nakedly show that, for ethnic Koreans who cross institutional borders, the Cold-War dichotomy of a divided country can be activated at anytime. Such over-reactions are a backlash to the institutional fluidity that resulted from increased mobility of diasporas, and to the breaking down of some of the North-South Korean borderlines that resulted in turn from such mobility and fluidity. Furthermore, these backlash responses are inversely proving that Korea is already a "border city." The nationalization project, the sate project of expanding the nation, that the Republic of Korea has been engaged in through the government's "monopoly over the legitimate means of movement" has now reached a critical point and is mutually incompatible with the dynamics that try to retrieve people back to their original places in the old order.

4. Border Ideology and Flexible Identity

As I have examined above, an acquisition of nationality is the practical and institutional borderline that Joseonjeok Zainichi Koreans must first overcome when they try to move to Korea. This reflects the colonialist and Cold War norms that have not disappeared even in an era of post-Cold War and globalization. Of course national borderlines are not the only lines of border there are: we repeat acts of drawing mental demarcations in our everyday activities. In other words, we form a circle around certain people, and in order to optimize the circle inside, we are habituated to acting to exclude all noises and risks. Zainichi Koreans are aware of the borderlines that South Korean society activates, as well as its dynamics of gaze. In other words, they are aware of the "borderline ideology" in South Korea and negotiate with them by way of compromising with, avoiding, resisting, and taking advantage of them. According to KWON Hyeok-tae, there are three filters through which Zainichi Koreans were represented in post-World War II Korea: developmentalism, anti-communism, and nationalism. Thus a Zainichi Korean was portrayed as either a "nouveau riche," a "commie," or a "half-Jap," respectively (KWON, 2007). What is at work here is the typology of historical consciousness according to which Zainichi Koreans have maintained close relationship with North Korea as they continued to live in the country of former colonial power that has since become a world economic power. Accordingly, the "pro-Japanese," "anti-Japanese," and "anticommunist" ideologies that shaped Korean society in the course of colonial rule and the North-South Korean division tend to wholly reflect themselves in South Koreans' perception of Zainichi Koreans. In this regard, South Koreas' perception of Zainichi Koreans is unique vis-à-vis other Korean diasporas; and the relationship of Zainichi Koreans to Korean society at large is distinct in this respect.

Of course, as we seen earlier, these basic frameworks have been in retreat clearly with the advance of a post-Cold War era, and there are now more holes through which one can escape the traps. In particular, the biggest change that came in 2000s is that formal and informal contacts between Chongryon-affiliated Zainichi and South Korean society have been increasing. LEE Nam-ji (Female, 42) married a South Korean man in the early 1990s and have been living in South Korea since 1996. She states that until the 1990s, a question always followed as to whether she was Mindan-affiliated or Chongryon-affiliated when she introduced herself as a Zainichi Korean. But according to her, the question disappeard in the 2000s, or that could perhaps be attributed to a generation difference. People over forty years of age always do the ideology check, "Which side are you?" National Security Law is still in effect in South Korea; the borderline dynamics is pregnant with opportunities to become activated anytime according to the changing political conditions. Under these circumstances, Chongryon-affiliated Zainichi Koreans in South Korea are self-aware of the positions they are in, and they try to find emotional links to Korean society by trying to correct their Korean school-style "Korean language" or by emphasizing that their ancestral home is in South Korea. The number of Zainichi women who are former students of Korean school, who marry Korean men, has seen an increase recently; these women do not reveal their past to their in-laws, their families, and friends around them in Korea. They are not hiding, but they feel they do not have to volunteer to draw lines that divide people.

Those with long-term experience of Korea take realistic and strategic communication modes. PARK Li-hye (Female, 35) has been living in Korea for eight years, and she can be either "a Korean" or "a Japanese." She divides and represents elements of herself according to whom she meets, but her identity belongs to the Korean school community that she grew up with. The co-existence of the freedom of representation and security of belongingness that she demonstrates shows "self-representation" is not the same as "identity." KANG Tae-hwan is also learning to represent himself in a broad range of ways. From the beginning, he was self-aware that he has many resources. When he is with friends who are fond of Japan, he can please them with his fluent Japanese; when he is with progressive South Korean activists, he can sing a North Korean song. He is learning to strategically negotiate with the Cold War/Division ideology; without distinguishing a South Korean gaze and 'self,' or representation and identity, he negotiates flexibly with multiple strata of people, as he takes on a flexible identity in the course. In other words, such flexibility of subject also signifies an alternative, an opposition to the institutional inflexibility he experienced in the course of acquiring Korean nationality.

5. Beyond the Dual Standard of 'National' vs. 'Multicultural'

In terms of everyday borderline, all Zainichi Koreans in Korea generally experience language and culture barriers. One word that is being widely circulated in Korea these days is "multiculturalism." However, the constituents of "multi-culture" as proposed by its proponents generally refer to migrant workers, and they do not include overseas Koreans who have South Korean nationality. Regardless of how culturally heterogeneous they are, the value conferred upon Zainichi Koreans is not "multicultural" but "national". In a public opinions survey led by YUN In-jin, 55.4% of the respondents said they felt positive about cultural diversity, while 62.9% also accepted pride in national homogeneity as positive (YUN et al., 2010: 113-114).[11] In other words, in Korea today, multiculturalism and nationalism are not at variance with one another; instead, they are being established as co-existing values. The fact that multiculturalism cannot replace nationalism in South Korea today is the limitation of the reality of North-South Korean division. The problem is that this dual standard of multiculturalism versus nationalism is applied arbitrarily in the form of "internalization" or "externalization." In other words, this dual standard does not challenge the "nationals vs. foreigners" or "us vs. others" dichotomy. One simply chooses one or the other side, depending on the circumstances.

Zainichi Koreans themselves are not entirely free from this kind of dichotomous perspective. The question of whether or not he or she can be recognized as a member of the Korean "nationals" is a life-consuming issue for a Zainichi Korean youth, and the question is accompanied by constant self-censorship. For generations in Japan, Zainichi Koreans have been treated as complete foreigners, and as the object of strict immigration control; they are sensitive to being treated as outsiders in South Korea. Most Zainichi Koreans, who first move to Korea to "learn the mother

11 Yun et al. (2010), 113-114.

language," often are disappointed by the ubiquitous double standard they find in South Korea; the disappointment can lead to a complete loss of meaning and a break-off of their will to stay in Korea. Even with the change of generations in South Korean society, such situations can repeat themselves. As can be seen in prior studies "hurt (*sangcheo*)," "disappointment," "betrayal," "alienation," and "unrequited love (*jjaksarang*)" are words that Zainichi Koreans often use to describe their experience in Korea. All interviewees interviewed for this study were self-aware of such "typified pattern," or the "disappointment course," and they were seeking ways to engage in different kinds of relations.

LEE Chang (Male, 50) learned elementary Korean in college, but he felt "a serious deficiency in national identity" and decided to come to Korea as a foreign student at age 40. He had worked as a reporter for a local newspaper in Japan with an annual salary of 100 million won, but he could not find meaning in mingling with the movers and shakers of the area and writing articles about it. Economically, his life is now much more unstable in comparison. However, by learning Korean, he is experiencing the "process of his deficient identity being filled." He is worried that he will forget Korean again if he returns to Japan, which is the reason for his staying in Korea now for the tenth year. But Korea is not at all a comfortable place for him; people are very opinionated, and loud, too, about it. It is also difficult for him to find a friend to talk to. Evaluating himself to be "closer to being a Japanese" than a Korean, he confessed that he is actually quite tired of living in Korea.

> After a few years, I came to see Korean society for what it is. I think it was good. It was a time when I came to actually viscerally experience, through my skin, what I had only abstractly thought of as "fatherland." I came to know. "Fatherland" is fatherland. It does not suit me, but it is what it is. The big gain here for me is that I can now accept it as is. Instead of simply revolting against it and returning to Japan, I have come to accept Korea for what it is, that it's like that. Not for me, but it's my fatherland. (LEE Chang).

He repeatedly emphasized that he was able to accept the "fatherland" as is when he broke out of thinking about it abstractly. It was in fact an acknowledgment that Japan, where he was born and grew up, was a country that was more comfortable for him. In the case of LEE Nam-ji who has been working as a Japanese instructor since the 1990s in Korea, she was self-aware that she and people like her have played a bridging role in advancing Korea-Japan relations as they have experienced social changes in South Korea as "border riders." At the same time, on the other hand, they were also asked, mostly in *hagwon*, to use a Japanese name; and in some colleges they were asked to not reveal that personal background as Zainichi Koreans and to work only as "a Japanese instructor." These practices still continue to this day.

> [They asked me] to pretend as if I were Japanese... In colleges it was okay to use my real name, but in *hagwon*, none of the places said it was okay. I usually check at the very beginning, if I could say that I am Zainichi. But then, none of the hagwon said that it was okay [...] It seemed to be at the discretion of the department chair, and at the beginning, I felt bad. Why did I have to use a Japanese name here in Korea... But, now I make the distinction and think that work is work. Actually, it seems that it's not the students themselves but their parents who prefer Japanese. They have faith in "natives" even though we are surely natives ourselves. (Lee Nam-ji, 42)

Because of this awkwardness, she chose to work for employers who preferred Zainichi Koreans, and she been using her own name at work for some time now. The Zainichi Koreans who have been working in the field of "language study," which presupposes a nation-state frame, have been the unsung heroes of Korea-Japan exchanges, as their identities have been glossed over as "the bridge" between the two countries. However, since the mid-2000s, the Korea-Japan cultural dynamics have changed, and while demand for learning Japanese by Koreans has decreased, demand by Japanese to learn Korean pop culture has increased dramatically. Among Zainichi Koreans living in Korea who have salaried jobs, they often work in areas that serve, either directly or indirectly, the cultural industry related to

Hallyu, or the Korean Wave. In the case of Choe Jun-hyeong, who came to Korea to learn Korean while he was still a graduate student in Japan, he has supported himself by making websites for information on Korea for Japanese browsers. He is grateful that he can support himself in Korea. That is because in Japan, with a degree in humanities, it is difficult to find a job even with a graduate school degree. The response of family and friends in Japan also changed dramatically. When Lee Nam-ji was leaving Japan to come to Korea with her Korean husband, family and friends dissuaded her saying, "You are a college graduate, how could you get married and go to such a backward country!" Now, their eyes sparkle with expectations, and they ask "How's Korea?"

Teaching Japanese in a language *hagwon* from the 1980s and 90s, and working as Japanese language staff in Hallyu-related jobs since the 2000s, have been the important means of livelihood for Zainichi living in Korea. The dual or the border-culture socio-cultural assets that they acquired in Japan have been re-contextualized as their means of survival in South Korea (KIM Ye-rim, 2009). On the subject of working with Japanese nationals at work, as "Jap- anese" themselves but with a Korean name, most of them feel just fine. As for "using" Japan as a means to earn a living, they accept that, too, as part of their identity. Instead, apart from work, they have a network of special and intimate Korean friends with whom they can fully share their identity; it is such a network that sustains their life and provide emotional stability in South Korea.

To them, in terms of living, and from the identity perspective, Korea and Japan are by no means mutually exclusive choices. Rather than "permanently settling" in one place, they wish to be able to go back and forth, and they take a transnational, trans-border space as their living space. For CHOE Jun-hyeong, who has been living in Korea now for a fifth year, Seoul has become a comfortable place for him, more so than any city in Japan he has not been acquainted with. Reversely, for LEE Nam-ji who lives thirty minutes away from the airport in Korea, going to Japan takes less time than going to Busan on KTX, the bullet train. Her in-laws tell her, who has been in Korea for fifteen years, to give up her Japanese permanent resident status and to become a "complete Korean" with the Korean national identification card. But She does not want abandon Japan, which is part of her. She knows very well that she cannot become a "complete Korean" even if she lives here longer than she has lived in Japan. In fact, she is aware that it is more realistic for her to take advantage of her in-between-ness and keep both the Korean and Japanese in her.

Zainichi Koreans live on the borders of both the "nation" and the "multiculture." A one-sided imposition forced on their life serves as an opportunity to indelibly imprint the asymmetry of their relationship with South Korean society. What is problematic here is not the demarcation itself, but that the lines are always imposed upon from without, regardless of his/her opinion, that they are drawn arbitrarily. In other words, the problem is that the criteria for drawing a line have always been outside of herself/himself. The presence of returning/migrating diasporas questions both the "nationalism" and the "multiculturalism" that is too "Republic-of-Korea-centered," and the strategic positions revealed by interviewees in this study show that such mediating practices are already possible. For them, by no means is Korea a land of "repatriation" only, not a place where they put all their takes in their identity only; instead, it is an extended space of living, it is becoming a space where they can transform their instability into positive resources.

6. Imaginary Move and Cultural Connection

Lastly, what I would like to examine is the cultural and emotional context of Zainichi Koreans who move to South Korea in a post-Cold War era. Hallyu dramatically transformed the cultural traffic of East Asia since the 2000s, and Zainichi Koreans were the engine behind Hallyu. An examination of this process reveals significant differences in their acceptance of Hallyu vis-à-vis Japanese. While most Zainichi Koreans in Japan have their family roots in what is now South Korea, for a long time the country remained for them only "an imaginary fatherland." In particular, for Chongryon-affiliated Zainichi, who were officially barred from visiting or having contacts with anyone in South Korea, the rise of Korean popular culture gave them an opportunity to realize that democratization in South Korea is real, and that a 'post-division' era is opening. Those who went to Korean schools had the language and cultural advantages to understand and be immersed in Korean popular culture. Contrary to the South Korean official image that they are ideologically enemies of the Republic of Korea, Chongryon-affiliated Zainichi are linguistically and emotionally equipped to readily make contacts with pro-democracy and pro-post-Cold War community in Korea. In other words, we can find an unintended effect of the non-divisional orientation of the Zainichi Koreans in their relationship with Korean society. Of the interviewees who attended the Korean schools in Japan, three had actively embraced Korean pop culture from the 1990s.

> Long before the Korean Wave came I was enjoying it on my own. I think I was in my 20s when I saw the Korean drama *War and Love* (Jeonjaeng gwa Sarang)... Have you seen it, by any chance? It was a love story between a former Partisan guerilla and a South Korean. The historical period [covered in the drama] coincided with the modern history we learned in school, and I really got into it. It was really real for me. My whole family watched it together, and then we gave the tapes to our relative. Of course our family also really got into watching *Hourglass* (Morye Sigye). So I got started early on the Internet, to find out, get more information about Korean dramas... Looking back, I think they helped a lot with my Korean and in familiarizing myself with Korean sensibilities. (YANG Mi-yeong, Female, 37)

> When I was in Japan, at home we had KNTV on all day, and my grandmother and father only watched Korean TV. When I first tried to go to

> Korea, it was to attend a fan meeting of a Korean star. I don't know when it all started, but... So when I first brought my prospective marriage partner (Korean) to Japan, the welcome response from my grandmother was overwhelming. I thought she would be opposed, but she was really pleased. Because he could speak "our language." All our relatives also really like it when my husband comes. They feel they are meeting "a real Korean," not a Korean through a screen. (PARK Li-hye, 35)

Formal releases of Korean dramas in the form of VHS or DVD began following the arrival of Hallyu in the mid-2000s. Until the 1990s, watching a Korean drama was possible only through the illegal video rental shops operated by Korean newcomers in Japan. According to Song Yeon-ok, it was around 1993 when video rental shops for Korean movies and dramas began sprouting rapidly in Imazato, Osaka, an area with heavy concentration Korean newcomers. Then Chongryon-affiliated Zainichi Koreans, the "old-comers," who had the money and the language, made forays into this market, and they quickly formed a major audience bloc (Song Eoun-ok, 2008: 240). With the opening of KNTV in 1996, it became possible to watch Korean TV in Japan. Most of the subscribers to the station, who had to pay 3,500 yen per month, were Koreans both old and new. That changed after 2004, when NHK showed the Korean drama *Winter Sonata* (Gyeoul Yeonga) to an explosive popular reception; Japanese subscribers now make up eighty percent of the KNTV subscription. A study has shown that before Hallyu, or "Korean wave," KNTV showed many documentary films on democratization of South Korea, but that after the arrival of Hallyu the cable TV has been focused on showing Korean melodramas and popular stars on entertainment programs (Song Eoun-ok, 2009: 243, Lee Hyang-jin, 2008: 78). For some Zainichi Koreans, the spread of the so-called "Japanese-style Hallyu" meant that Korean modern and contemporary history, which made it possible for them to come in contact with Korean society for the first time, became less "real." KIM So-won (Female, 45), whom I interviewed in Japan, brushed up on her Korean pronunciations by watching Korean dramas long before they became "a wave."

> It began with "*Hourglass* (Morye Sigye)" of course... My mother and I stayed up all night watching it. I thought, wow, they could portray Gwangju this way. It was new, and it was moving. The music filled my heart, the characters were completely believable, and more than anything else, the language... It stirred an intense desire in me to speak "our language," a language like that. From then on I made sure to get hold every Korean drama available, and I began my Korean blog before 2000. At the time, for me, the browser, the square of the computer, was Korea itself. (KIM So-won, Female, 45)

Kim So-won graduated from a Korean high school in 1987. She kept pace with political discourses in Korea in real time, and she has the memory of sharing the turbulent time with democratization forces in South Korea. She visited Korea for the first time in 2000 and by chance met Korean artist-activists. Since then she has been in contact with them through an on-line network. They understood her Joseonjeok status and have been very supportive of her. Through her experience with them, she is confident that she has seen "ordinary Korean citizens who are dedicated and ethical." The on-line communication she has with them is also an opportunity for her to improve her Korean. What is currently substituting her move to Korea is her relationship with Korean foreign students in Japan. She has conversations in Korean with them and learns about Korean food and culture; she experiences "surrogate Korea" with them. The changes since 2000 have been visceral, and she describes them as follows:

> Until the early 1990s, my only reason for wanting to go to Korea was the thought that "I want participate in the democratization process with them." Purely political... But since the 2000s, I really want to go to Korea not just for a political reason, but to experience the culture, the emotions, and everyday living... To me, it is not "the Republic of Korea," but Seoul, Gwang-ju, or Jeju Island that I want to go... Of course, there are people who say "We will never go there as long as the National Security Act is still in force." But I think it is nonsense to see the present, the 2000s, with the 80s lens. I know how much sacrifice there has been, and I want to visit Korea out

> of respect for them, and I want to be where they are still breathing. (KIM So-won)

Kim, who went to Korean schools and graduated from a Korean university, had a much more intimate relationship with North Korea in her formative years, in comparison to Zainichi Koreans in general. However, speaking of herself now, she says that North Korea is becoming the subject of nostalgia, and that there is lack of cultural-emotional attachment with it. In other words, the Korean language, the sense of national identity, the historical consciousness, and the cultural and emotional resources that she cultivated formerly as a student in Korean schools are now being re-affirmed and re-built through her new relationship with people in South Korea. This phenomenon is not limited only to Kim So-won or the other interviewees in this study. Zainichi Koreans who work in language-related or Korean-culture related jobs—as well as the countless Korean school graduates who embrace the Korean Wave—are re-building, in a South Korean context, their cultural assets, both linguistic and emotional, that they have acquired through "Korean education" from their childhood. As if in an inverse proportion to the increasing opportunities they have in making contacts in South Korea, North Korea, which had close ties with them originally, is becoming further and further demonized in Japanese society (Kim, 2011). Thus the status of Chongryon-affiliated Zainichi Koreans shows where Cold War intersects post-Cold War, which does not necessarily mean that their positions have changed from "Joseon" to "Republic of Korea." The past and present constantly negotiate with one another, forming individual identities that are complex.

The experiences of Zainichi Koreans described in this chapter by no means apply to Zainichi Koreans in general. Not all Zainichi Koreans give priority to a national identity in embracing the Korean Wave. However, the Zainichi migration to South Korea in the post-Cold War era, and their embracement of Korean popular culture, is informed by their history and experiences, both formal and informal, of not giving up their ties with the "home country (bonguk)." It is perhaps only natural that Chongryon-affiliated Zainichi, whose disposition from the very beginning were non-Divisional, actively sought out ties with South Korean society even as they kept close ties with North Korea. It is not their ideology, nor their place of belongingness, that moved from "Joseon" to "Hanguk;" what has shifted is the firmness of the boundaries within us. Living in a globalizing world, we move constantly even as we physically stay stationary (Bauman, 1998), and the imaginary power of movement cannot forcibly be confined by a past regime. The case of Kim So-won in this study, in particular, shows how the physical restriction of movement only makes the imagination more fertile.

7. Concluding Remarks

I have examined above, through the cases of second- and third-generation Zainichi moving to Korea mostly after the post-Cold War period, the boundaries, ideological and otherwise, that they face in everyday living, and how they negotiate with them. What was found commonly among them is that Korea is not a place they return to stake their national identity only; instead, Korea is also a place where they find out about and affirm the cultural assets of the border identity that they have. Almost all the interviewees distanced themselves from the expression "repatriation," making their return/migration a special choice in the context of their historical memory. The return/migration of diasporas inevitably connects them to history and to reinterpret it, and the method of the connection is very complex. Here, perhaps, we can see the dynamism of history and reality in which the consequences of the diasporas experience of the past have made the trans-border acts and the trans-border mode of being possible in the present.

Given that South Korean institutions and customs strictly divide nationals vs. foreigners and nation vs. multiculture, the reality of the Zainichi Koreans in movement suggests a need to approach them as not only "repatriates," or returning diasporas, but as trans-cultural "migrants." This is not to suggest that the "multi-culture" policy in Korea simply include overseas Koreans as part of multi-culture groups in Korea. Contrary to it, it is to suggest that the problem of multiculturalism in Korea, which advocates "Koreanization of foreigners," be critically reflected upon through the examples of the diasporas. In other words, the mutually exclusive categories of "nation" and "multiculture" are not what is needed; what is needed is a shift in perception where a "nation" is understood as being multicultural by nature, and where "compatriot (*dongpo*)" is understood as a moving entity, a hybrid in itself that has many boundaries within itself.

Furthermore, Zainichi Koreans who are not moving, or whose movement is blocked, are not outside of the theme of the diasporas movement; their course of cultural-emotional connections to South Korea have shaped the conditions and provided the foundation for another important movement. In the case of the Korean school graduates, in particular, who have the linguistic cultural asset, they remain physically in Japan, but their imaginary movement is all the more active. It is in this context that this chapter focuses on Chongryon-affiliated Zainichi, who are a minority. I leave the detailed discussion of the composition of the Zainichi population and the distinctions among various Zainichi populations to a future task. An examination of the lives of diasporas in movement is important in shedding light on the discussion of Korean diasporas, the North-South Korea Division, and the "multi-culture" discourse, and in showing that they are inextricably bound together.

Bibliography

Appadurai, Arjun (1996), *Modernity at large: Cultural Dimensions of Globalization*, University of Minnesota Press.

Baumen, Zygmunt (1998), *Globalization: The Human Consequences*, Polity Press.

Brubaker, Rogers (2005), "The 'diasporas' diasporas," *Ethnic and Racial Studies*, 28(1).

CHO Kyung-hee (2007), "*Hanguk sahoeui jaeil joseonin insik* (Korean Perception of Zainichi Koreans)," *Hwanghae Review* (Hwanghae Munhwa), Winter.

Clifford, James (1997), "Diaspora," *Routes, Travel and Translation in the Late Twentieth Century*, Harvard University Press.

Hall, Stuart (1990), "Cultural Identity and Diaspora," *Identity: Community, Culture, Difference*, London: Lawrence & Wishart.

HAN Tong-hyun (2004), "Kankoku drama 'Morye sigye' to chosen gakkou shussinsha, 386 sedai tono Doukeisei wo Megutte" (Korean Drama, *Hourglass* and Korean Ethnic Shool Graduates: Isomorphism with 386 Generation in South Korea), *Gendai-Shiso* (Contemporary Philosophy), 34(4).

HAN Yeong-gu *et al.* (2003), Hyeondae Hanil gwangye Jaryojip (Resource Book on Contemporary Korea-Japan Relations). Vol. 1 (1965-1979), Oreum.

HAN Young-hae (2011), "Zaikan-Zainichi Chosenjin, hongoku tono atarashii kankei: 'Chosen' kara 'Kankoku' ni 'Kokuseki Henkou' sita Zainichi 3sei wo chosin ni" (Zainichi Koreans in South Korea, New Relationship with Homeland: Focusing on third generation who changed Nationality to 'South Korea' from 'Korea'), *Migration Policy Review*, No. 3.

KWON Suk-in (2008), "Diaseupora jaeil haninui 'gwihan' (The

"Repatriation" of Diaspora Zainichi Koreans)." *The International Area Review* (Gukje jiyeok yeongu), 17(4).

KWON Hyeok-tae (2007), "Jaeil Joseonin gwa Hanguk saehoe: Hanguk saehoeneun jaeil joseonineul eotteoke 'pyosang' hae wanneunga (Zainichi Koreans and Korean Society: How has Korean society "represented" Zainichi Koreans)." *Yuksa bipyung* (History Critique), Spring.

KIM Tae-sik (2011), "Bundan sareru Zainichi Chosenjin"(Divided Zainichi Koreans), *Impaction*, No. 180.

KIM Yerim (2009), "Idonghaneun gukjeok, weolgyeonghaneun juche, gyeongyeejeok munhwa jabon: Hangungne jaeil joseionin 3 (sam)seui jeongcheseong jeongchiwa munhwa heyonsil (Nationality in movement, Subjects in border-transgression, and Borderline Cultural Assets: Border Politics of 3rd-Generation Zainichi in South Korea and Their Cultural Practices)." Sangheo Hakbo, No. 25.

LEE Hyang-jin, translation by Shimizu Yukiko (2008), *Kanryu no shakaigaku: fandom, kazoku, ibunka-koryu* (Sociology of Hallyu: Fandom, Family, Cross-Cultural Communication), Iwanami Shoten.

Ryang, Sonia (2002), "Diaspora and Beyond: There is No Home for Koreans in Japan," *Review of Korean Studies*, 4(2), 55-86.

Safran, William (1991), "Diasporas in modern societies: Myths of homeland and return," *Diaspora*, 1(1), 83-99.

SEO Gyeong-sik, translation by KWON Heok-tae (2011), *Eoneoui gamokeseo* (In the Prison of Language), Dolbege.

Sheffer, Gabriel (2003), *Diaspora Politics at Home Abroad*, Cambridge University Press.

SONG Eoun-ok (2008), "Zanishi Chosenjin ni totte no 'Kanryu'" (Hallyu for Zainichi Koreans), Seo Sung *et al.* *'Kanryu' no Uchi Soto: Kankoku Bunka-ryoku to Higashi ajia no Yugou Hannou* (In and Out of 'Hallyu': Korean Cultural Power and Fusion Reaction of East-Asia), Ochanomizu

Shobo.

Torpey, J. (2000), The *Invention of Passport: Surveillance, Citizenship*, State. Cambridge University Press.

YUN In-jin, SONG Yeong-ho, KIM Sang-don, and SONG Ju-yeong (2010), *Hanguginui iju nodongjawa damunhwa sahoe e daehan insik* (Koreans' Perception of Migrant Workers and Multi-cultural Community), Idam.

4

The Cultural Politics of Communication and Difference:

A Case Study of the Chinese-Korean Community in South Korea

by LEE Jeong-eun

Humanities Korea Research Professor
Institute for East Asian Studies at SungKongHoe University

1. Introduction

The South Korean Law on Overseas Korean Immigration and Legal Status (Jaeoe dongpo ui churipguk gwa beopjeok jiwi e gwanhan beomnyul) was revised in 2005; the "guest worker" program went into effect as of March 2007; and the number of Joseonjok[i], now living in South Korea, has reached over 400,000. With these changes, the day-to-day world of the Joseonjok has also been undergoing transformation.[1] However, general preju-

i Ethnic Koreans in China are referred to as Joseonjok, literally "the Joseon tribe" or "the people of Joseon." The term reflects large-scale historical settlements of Korean population in Northeast China prior to 1945–translator.

1 As of December 2010, there are 415,000 Chinese-Koreans in South Korea, and this number represents 87% of all Koreans with foreign nationalities (*oeguk gukjeok dong-po*) residing in the country. Of the Chinese-Koreans mentioned, 286,586 are staying

dice against Chinese-Koreans in South Korea is similar vis-a-vis other "guest workers." The fact that Chinese-Koreans speak Korean has not been a factor in increasing cultural understanding between the Chinese-Korean community and the South Korean public at large; instead, it has served as an incentive for a distinct form of discrimination against Chinese-Koreans, and this has led to a strong and deep sense of "betrayal" on the part of Chinese-Koreans in South Korea.[2] These Chinese-Koreans[ii] are certainly "foreigners," but because they are *dongpo*[iii] who share the same blood lineage, the Chinese-Koreans wish to be treated differently vis-a-vis other guest workers in South Korea. They also complain that the South Korean government's immigration policy is discriminatory in that it treats Chinese-Koreans unfairly in comparison to overseas Koreans coming from other countries such as the United States, for example.

Thus, there is a perceptual gap in how Chinese-Koreans and

---

in the country on the Guest Worker (H2) visa. See "Oeguk gukjeok dongpo hyeonhwang" (Current Status of Overseas Korean Immigration) on *E-nara jipyo* (e-national indexes), an on-line national statistics information system (www.index.go.kr). See also KIM Hyeon-mi (2009) for a study of the day-to-day world of Chinese-Korean Guest Workers in South Korea.

2 In South Korea, Koreans with Chinese nationality are called by many names. In general, they are referred to as Joseonjok. Other appellations include *Jungguk dongpo, Jaehan dongpo*, and *Jaejung dongpo*, (which are all a variation of "Chinese-Koreans living in South Korea" -Tr.). In this paper they are referred to as *Jaejung dongpo*, which is an abbreviation of *Jaehan Jungguk dongpo*, which the Korean government began to use officially since the introduction of the 2007 guest worker program. Depending on the context, they will also be referred to as Joseonjok and other appellations mentioned above.

ii The English translation "Chinese-Korean(s)" in this chapter refers to "Chinese-Korean(s) living in South Korea," unless otherwise noted -Tr.

iii A literal translation of *dongpo* in English is "compatriot(s)." Generally, it is also accurate to translate it as "overseas Korean(s)" or "ethnic Korean(s)." It is also possible to translate *dongpo* as "overseas Korean(s) with foreign/Korean nationality." Thus, *Jungguk* (Chinese) *dongpo*, for example, can be translated as "Korean compatriot(s) living in China," "overseas Korean(s) living in China," or "ethnic Korean(s) living China." Here, it will be translated as "Chinese-Korean(s)"—with the hyphen—for the sake of brevity and ease of recognition, along with the other terms. Also, the term Joseonjok, which can be used interchangeably with *Jungguk dongpo*, will not be separately translated -Tr.

South Korean society at large see each other. If one were to look at the cause of this difference from a discursive perspective, one observes that the Chinese-Korean argument is based on a strong "*minjok* (nation) discourse." On the other hand, a "multiculturalism discourse," an attempt to overcome the boundary of nationality or nation, is currently widespread in South Korea. One reason for the perceptual difference here is that the point of contact between these two discourses is not very large. The criticism and complaint on the part of the Chinese-Koreans that South Koreans are not properly treating their "compatriots" (*gateun minjok*) or their "own people" (*uri dongpo*) do not have much common ground with the scattered local attempts to promote multiculturalism. Such attempts include programs that may bear titles such as "Learning About Other Cultures" (*Ta munhwa alligi*) and "Learning Korean Culture" (*Hanguk munhwa baeugi*). The current multiculturalism discussions in South Korea do not adequately address the complex cultural dynamics of migration and settlement, during the courses of which cultures are newly created or transformed; instead, the current discourse tends to make the already existing nation-state boundaries further entrenched.

Neo-liberal globalization is accelerating international migration of labor, and entrenched social boundaries are being further reinforced through discourse politics in South Korea. Under these circumstances, one of the practical reasons for the deepening division between South Korean society and Chinese-Korean community at large is that there is no concrete venue where the two communities can communicate with each other. Where is the possibility? Where can Chinese-Koreans communicate with South Koreans, not as workers confined to the rigid employer-employee framework, and not as the Otherized "they" of the Guro-Garibong area—the leading population center of the Chinese-Korean migrants in South Korea[iv]—but as the subject, the princi-

iv Guro refers to Guro-gu, and Garibong refers to Garibong-dong, which is part of ple party of interest, representing itself in the dialogue?

I propose to find one such possibility in small-group meetings, organizations, and networks organized by Chinese-Koreans. Accordingly, this chapter focuses on how Chinese-Koreans, as they migrate to South Korea, develop networks for human and material exchanges. In particular, this study focuses on exchanges taking place among Chinese-Korean communities in South Korea, and on how Chinese-Koreans come in contact with South Korean society at large, and the course of their engagement with mainstream South Korean society beyond the local boundaries of their own migrant population centers.

Community studies on Joseonjok society have thus far mostly dealt with Joseonjok communities and their urban cultures in China.[3] More recently, with a rapid increase of Chinese-Korean population in South Korea, interest has been rising on studying their migrant population centers in South Korea; also, new attempts are being made to study how Chinese-Koreans in South Korea have come to form a significant labor force in the country; there has also been research interest in Chinese-Koreans who have migrated to a third country.[4] It should also be noted that, in terms of studies so far on Joseonjok migrants in South Korea, their migration paths and networking courses are somewhat well-documented; however, few researchers have studied their local communities and analyzed their organizational and small-group activities.[5]

Geumcheon-gu. The author's reference to the Guro-Garibong area also loosely includes Daerim-dong, which is part of Yeongdeungpo-gu –Tr.

3 On this, see YUN In-jin (2003); KWON Tae-hwan and PARK Kwang-seong (2004); PARK Myeong-gyu (2005); PARK Kwang-seong (2006); and YE Dong-geun (2009).

4 For studies on Chinese-Korean population centers, see KIM Hyeon-seon (2010); PARK Se-hoon (2010); and IM Seon-il (2010). On the formation of Chinese-Korean labor population in South Korea, see YI Jin-yeong and PARK U (2009); On Joseonjok who migrated to England, see KIM Hyeon-mi (2008).

5 On Joseonjok migration paths and networking, see KWON Tae-hwan (2003); YI Jin-yeong and PARK U (2009); and KIM Hyeon-mi (2008). On the possibility of Chinese-

The purpose of this chapter is to analyze the characteristics, mode, and content of various social exchanges in which the Chinese-Koreans engage in South Korea—keeping in mind that Korean society will become culturally more diversed with the acceleration of cross-border labor migration worldwide—and to reflect upon the strategies and positions of Chinese-Koreans in South Korea as they deploy "politics of difference."

2. Methodology

This chapter is based on participation-observation and in-depth interviews for collecting research data. To identify how communities are formed within the Chinese-Korean society in South Korea, and how they communicate with South Korean society at large—in other words, to identify the topography of their communities and their communication strategies—I participated in relevant community events and meetings. Also, local Chinese-Korean residents of the Guro, Daerim, Garibong neighborhoods,[6] as well as heads and members of their local community organizations were interviewed. Interviewees were selected through the "snowball sampling" method, and they were introduced to the researcher by local business owners and leaders of community organizations.

In selecting the interviewees, the goal was to match the population proportion of the Joseonjok in South Korea. However, given the daily living cycle of the workers, it was difficult to meet that goal. Joseonjok mostly work in "3D" ("Dirty, Dangerous, and Difficult/Demeaning") jobs, and their work hours are usually long. It meant that it was difficult to conduct interviews

Korean groups forming an alliance, see MUN Min (2010). On the "recognition struggle" of Joseonjok groups, see PARK U (2011).

6 Some Chinese-Koreans live in Ansan, Gyeonggi Province and in the Dongdaemun, Sinchon, and Jayang-dong areas in Seoul. However, the three neighborhoods of Guro, Daerim, and Garibong in Seoul have the largest concentrations of Joseonjok population, and thus was the reason for selecting interviewees from these areas.

with them in stable conditions. The most accessible interviewees were those who owned their own business. I interviewed them during slow-business hours, and I was also introduced to family members who worked with them.

Apart from the small-business owners, those with whom long interviews were possible were people with contractual jobs, people who were being treated for an illness, or construction laborers who were on rainy season hiatus. The interviews were conducted from February to August 2011, and in-depth interviews were carried out with heads and members of Chinese-Korean organizations and groups, as well as with journalists covering the local Joseonjok community.

<Table 1> Interviewees

No.	Code	Sex	Birth Year	Entry Year	Visa Type	Occupation in China	Current Occupation	Birth Place	Remarks
1	A	F	1960	2008	H2	Service industry	Caretaker for the sick	Tumen	Family invitation
2	B	M	1951	2008	H2	Farmer	Construction day laborer	Yanbian	Construction site in Daegu
3	C	M	1964	2000	H2	Bank	Constructin day laborer	Yanji	Undocum ented
4	D	F	1953	2007	H2	Women's Committee, Local head	Live-in housework	Yanji	Family invitation
5	E	F	1948	2007	H2	Food factory worker	Live-in housework	Tumen	Family invitation
6	F	F	1954	2005	H2	Department store clerk	Live-in housework	Hunchun	Family invitation
7	G	F	1949	2007	H2	Tap water inspector	Live-in housework	Heilong-jian Province	Old
8	H	M	1965	2010	H2	Farming, construction	Construction day laborer	Longjing	Korean language test
9	I	F	1953	2008	H2	Nurse	Caretaker for the sick	Yanji	Family invitation
10	J	M	1937	1994	H2	Civil servant	Interpretation, translation	Tumen	Undocum ented, Old

11	K	F	1950	2007	H2	Railroad worker	Caretaker for the sick	Longjing	Family invitation
12	L	M	1957	2009	H2	Civil servant	Kitchen aide	Yanji	Family invitation
13	M	M	1966	2008	H2	Farming, moving	Construction day laborer	Yanbian	Korean language test
14	N	F	1945	1997	H2	Farming	Live-in housework	Yanbian	Family invitation, Aged
15	O	M	1952	2007	H2	Charcoal factory	Electronic communica-tions	Longjing	Family invitation
16	P	F	1954	2007	H2	Housework	Small business	Yanji	Family invitation
17	Q	F	1957	1998	Korean	Housework	Small business	Yanji	Marriage
18	R	M	1971	1997	E9	Teacher	Small business	Shenyang	Undocum ented
19	S	M	1960	1993	F4	Labor	Small business	Tumen	Undocum ented
20	T	M	1981	2003	F4	College student	Graduate student	Longjing	Foreign student
21	U	F	1954	1997	Korean	Publishing company	Small business	Yanji	Naturalized
22	V	F	1952	1993	F4	Store clerk	Organization activist	Longjing	Undocum ented

3. Community Formation Utilizing Cultural Resources

1) Settlement in a Working-Class Neighborhood

The Chinese-Korean population in South Korea today is distributed throughout the country. In particular, they have been filling labor shortages in farming and fishing villages, and the proportion of their labor population is high in these rural villages and in local towns. The Joseonjok who work in farming and fishing villages upon entering South Korea for the first time are people who do not have contacts in South Korea. There are leaflets and other forms of direct advertisement targeting this population. It is through such advertising materials that the Joseonjok move out of the farming or fishing villages and into town jobs in local areas. There they become more familiar with goings-on in Korea and are exposed to active exchanges of information with other Chinese-Koreans, and they then move to the Seoul and Gyeonggi area where there are more job choices and wages are relatively higher. That is why approximately 170,000 of them, approximately 50% of all Chinese-Koreans in South Korea, live in the city of Seoul.

<Table 2> Number of Residents in Seoul Municipal Districts with Major Concentration of Chinese-Korean Population, 2006-2010 (Persons)

Municipal District (Seoul)	2006	2007	2008	2009	2010
Yeongdeungpo-gu	18,242	27,775	32,049	32,688	35,400
Guro-gu	14,933	22,256	25,398	25,172	26,381
Gwanak-gu	8,331	12,465	14,155	14,018	14,476
Geumcheon-gu	8,404	12,959	15,573	16,137	17,177
Gwangjin-gu	4,630	7,044	8,269	8,542	8,896
Dongjak-gu	4,948	7,048	7,929	7,749	8,067
Total	59,488	89,547	103,373	104,306	110,397
City Total	105,178	150,270	169,385	166,413	170,125
Country Total	236,854	328,621	376,563	377,560	409,079
Guro &Yeongdeungpo Districts/City (%)	31.5%	33.3%	34%	34.8%	36.3%

Source: Reconstructed from *Churipguk tonggye yeonbo* (Annual report on immigration statistics), 2006-2010.

<Table 2> shows that, of all the Chinese-Koreans living in Seoul, 36.3% live in Guro-gu and Yeongdeungpo-gu. The concentration of Joseonjok population in a few municipal districts (*gu*) in Seoul reflects a universal phenomenon of migration in which trans-border migration takes root with specific migrant population centers; a migrant population comes to settle in the destination country as the population builds economic spheres of its own around such population centers.

Population centers for migrant Chinese-Koreans have been built around Guro-gu, Yongdeungpo-gu, and Geumcheon-gu in Seoul because these areas, as a whole, have particular historical-geographical characteristics. When Korea first opened its ports to foreign countries at the end of the 19th century, the present-day Guro area served as a midpoint connecting the port of Jemulpo in Incheon and Seoul. Thus, more than a century ago, it became a traffic hub for humans and goods. After national liberation in 1945, many who escaped from the north, as well as those returning to Korea from abroad, settled in this area. After the Korean War, when the armistice agreement was signed, population in the area increased again, because it was the cross-point between Seoul and Incheon. In the 1960s, an industrial complex for export industries was built in the area, and young female factory workers began moving there in large numbers. At the end of the 1980s, South Korean industrial structure was re-organized, and heavy chemical industry became a dominant national industry. Manufacturing companies moved their factories overseas, and for a time Guro suffered a severe reduction (a "hollowing out phenomenon") in residential population. Since then, Guro has been revived as a district that represents working-class culture and consciousness (LEE Mi-ae, 2008: 41-42).

Thus historically, population shift has been a prominent characteristic of Guro; its name is strongly associated with the working class, and it is known as one of the most notorious slum neighborhoods in Seoul. Since the 1990s, "foreigner workers" (*oegugin nodongja*) and Josenjok have been filling the hollowed out residential neighborhood. That is because migrant workers in Korea were moving toward industrial complexes in the Seoul metropolitan area, and Chinese-Korean workers remained in the Guro-Garibong neighborhood because rental fees are relatively cheaper and the neighborhood has good public transportation. The area still maintains many of the "beehive" housing structures that were built in the 1960s to accommodate the influx of young factory workers, and thus the rental fee in the neighborhood is still cheaper than in most areas in Seoul. Joseonjok began arriving in South Korea in the early 1990s. Many of them incurred debt to come to South Korea on a family invitation, on an official visit, as tourists, or in a disguised marriage. Low rent was a strong factor pulling them to the neighborhood.

More recently, many Joseonjok business and community establishments—restaurants, currency exchanges, small group meetings, community organizations and newspaper companies—have been set up in the area so that one is tempted to call it "Little Yanbian," and the area is fast becoming the hub of Joseonjok community life in South Korea. The neighborhood has become a venue for representing and experimenting with the notion of the "Joseonjok Community," as some Joseonjok in South Korea want to build a Jungguk Dongpo Town (Chinese-Korean Town), or Dongpo Town in short, that is different from "Chinatown."

2) Utilization of Cultural Resources and Reproduction of Boundaries

In cross-border migrations, social networking constitutes a very important mechanism. For migrants who are looking for a better life in the globalizing market economy, and whose only weapon is their labor power, information about, and social and economic networking in, their destination country play a role of paramount importance in the course of their migration.[7]

In the case of Joseonjok, the major cultural asset that they consider to be important in deciding to come to South Korea is the language. The fact that they are fluent in "Joseon language" gives them the expectation that it will reduce the difficulty of

7 See Im Seon-il (2010) for the migration and cultural adaptation of ethnic Korean workers in South Korea and the transformation of ethnicity thereof.

settling down in South Korea. The language thus becomes a real resource in deciding to come to South Korea. In the case of "S" who is a business owner in Daerim-dong, the fact that he is fluent in "Joseon language" played the most import role in his decision to choose South Korea, and not some other countries, for migration.

Apart from "freedom of communication," another important factor for Chinese-Koreans in choosing to come to South Korea is the human network. It includes family, friends, people from the same region in China, and alumni groups. They operate as information-sharing networks for migration and adaptation in South Korea. When a Joseonjok woman who marries a Korean man, or a married man who enters South Korea as an undocumented worker, has spent a certain period time enough to settle down in Korea, he or she invites family members from China. At times, such networking has led to a veritable population shift where there are enough Chinese-Koreans from a single region that they can hold a class reunion in Seoul.

"Q" married a Korean man and came to South Korea in 1998, and she currently owns a restaurant in Daerim-dong. Her two sisters and their families have also moved to Daerim-dong in 2007. In the case of "S," he had been undocumented when he was deported to China in 1993. Since then he came back to South Korea on an invitation by family. Since his move back to Korea, he has invited his brother in law's family. He currently owns a small business.

In the cases of both Q and S, their migration typifies networking based on family ties. What they also share in common is that they are both early migrants to Korea; this means that they have information resources that others may lack and they now have enough of an economic footing to open a restaurant. On the other hand, many Chinese-Koreans who come to South

Korea on a family invitation visa work as day laborers. In a Chinese-Korean community, owning a small business means that the owner enjoys a certain social and economic stature in the community, and local networking takes place with them at the center.

S's wife runs their restaurant by herself, and S works as a day laborer on construction jobs "in order to earn more money." He gives practical help to his former classmates in finding work and places to live in South Korea. The classmates gather at his restaurant whenever they can, regardless of the day of the week, to soothe their loneliness by drinking together, or to hold regular group meetings. Such networking makes the reunion of Joseonjok classmates by school possible, which in turn becomes a foundation of forming a larger organization, like the Joseonjok association at a national level.

These networking activities have a positive role in sharing common experiences and providing assistance to those who need it in adapting to a new country. However, they also have a negative effect of deepening suspicions against South Koreans and prevent Joseonjok from adapting to South Korea (KIM Yeonggyeong, 2008: 175). In these cases, the migrants feel that they do not have to be in contact with South Koreans and experience discrimination and pain, when they can work and spend leisure time in the comfort of their own community.

4. Change from "Collective Political Action" to Routine Activities

1) From Church-based leadership to Self-based leadership

Chinese-Koreans who come to South Korea want to expand their contacts as they utilize the networks built during the course of their migration and participate in various community activities.

By participating in various gatherings, they share information on everyday living, cope with their loneliness, and form a community consensus. They are very vocal to protect their rights and interests, and it is said that "when five people get together, all five [become] the group head."

Discussions on the issues of protecting Chinese-Korean rights and interests began in the early 1990s with the support of religious organizations, at a time when many Chinese-Koreans were in South Korea as undocumented workers. The discussions took place within the framework of protecting the human rights of guest workers in general. Then, in 1999, the Law on Overseas Korean Immigration and Legal Status (in short, Jaeoe dongpo beop, or "Law on Overseas Koreans" –Tr.) was passed. The provisions of the law excluded Chinese-Koreans. Since then, the discussion of Chinese-Korean issues has taken place outside of the guest worker framework; instead, it has now become part of the "*minjok* discourse" or "*dongpo* discourse." Here again, religious organizations played a major role in lending support to Chinese-Korean workers.

Joseonjok organizations began moving away from church organizations and organizing on their own since the Law on Overseas Koreans was revised in 2005. The Chinese-Koreans whose statuses became legal after the revision of the Law became independent from religious organizations, or they formed their own organizations to protect their rights and interests. <Table 3> shows that it has not been quite ten years since many of the Chinese-Korean organizations in South Korea were established. There are many smaller organizations in local areas that are not listed on the table, but their activities are similar. They provide legal aid and labor counseling, support in settling down, and opportunities for social gathering.

This chapter will now examine the activities of two organi-

<Table 3> Chinese-Korean Organizations in South Korea

Organization	Year Established	Major Concerns
Chinese Workers Association (Jungguk nodongja hyeophoe)	1995	Provide free legal counseling: for women who have been victimized; divorce proceedings; fraud charges; civil and criminal cases; human rights violations; delayed wage and severance payments; compensation for workplace accidents and disasters; wrongful dismissals from job, etc.
Joseonjok Alliance (Joseonjok yeonhaphoe)	2000	Organize activities to revise Law on Overseas Koreans; operate "Urijip" (Our House), a shelter.
KCN: Network of Chinese-Korean Students in Korea (Jaehan Joseonjok yuhaksaeng neteuweokeu)	2003	Organize seminar series; promote lateral solidarity among foreign students.
Federation of Repatriating Overseas Koreans (Gwihwan dongpo yeonhap chonghoe)	2005	Provide support for settling down in South Korea to those who have acquired South Korean citizenship; educate on naturalization; operate a government-designated support center for Chinese-Koreans staying in South Korea.
Chinese-Korean One Mind Association (Jungguk dongpo hanmaeum hyeophoe)	2006	Offer volunteer activities for crime prevention; organize *cheyuk daehoe* ("sports day"); sponsor a calligraphy club, etc.
Korea-China Economic Friendship Exchange Association (Han-Jung gyeongjae chinseon gyoryu hyeophoe)	2007	Invite Chinese-Korean children for cultural exploration; advocate for policy changes impacting Chinese-Koreans in Korea; visa counseling.
Federation of Overseas Koreans in South Korea (Jaehan dongpo yeonhap chonghoe)	2008	Help with various grievances; provide counseling on immigration affairs; offer labor counseling and information.
Committee on Improving Lives of Naturalized Citizens (Gukjeok chwideukja saenghwal gaeseon wiwonhoe)	2009	Advocate for legislation to improve livelihoods of those who have received South Korean citizenship, first-generation Chinese-Koreans, and their children in South Korea.
Assembly of Chinese Federation Daegyeong Association of Overseas Exchanges (Jungguk yeonmaeng chonghoe Dae gyeong haewoe gyoryu hyeophoe)	2010	Advocate for justice on behalf of Chinese nationals, the overseas Chinese, and Chinese-Koreans living in South Korea; help those facing hardships, and provide free counseling and other services.

Source: Reconstructed from MIDRI REPORT. See "Jaehan Jungguk dongpo danche hyeonhwang gwa gwaje" (Current Status of Chinese-Korean Organizations in South Korea and Their Challenges), 75.

zations from the list of organizations in <Table 3> in a more detailed way. The first is the Joseonjok Alliance, an advocacy group for rights and interests of Joseonjok that is independent from a church organization, and the second is the Network of Chinese-Korean Students in Korea (KCN), which is a volunteer organization organized by young people. We will see how Joseonjok foreign students, who are relatively young compared to other Joseonjok in South Korea and are part of the intelligentsia in the community, utilize their community space and communicate with society at large in South Korea.

(1) Self-Organizations of Chinese-Korean Rights and Interests

Two organizations can be cited as the leading self-representative organizations for Chinese-Korean rights and interests in South Korea. They are the Joseonjok Alliance and the Federation of Overseas Koreans in South Korea. The Alliance began as a church-based organization and eventually became independent, while the Federation began as a self-representative organization from the start. Apart from this difference, there is also a class-composition difference. The main organizers of the Alliance are mostly workers in 3D industries, whereas the Federation is organized by small business owners in the Daerim-dong area.

Considering that church organizations still play a major role in the lives of Chinese-Koreans in South Korea, the fact that the members of the Alliance separated themselves from the church and established an organization to advocate their rights and interests on their own is a significant move within the Chinese-Korean community at large in South Korea. This organization was launched in 2000 with the support from Uijuro Church in Hongje-dong, Seodaemun-gu, Seoul. Most of the members of the Alliance at the time were undocumented, and they were helped by the Joseonjok Welfare Center, an organ of the church.

From the very beginning, the Alliance demanded "revision of

the Law on Overseas Koreans, amnesty for the undocumented, and guarantee of completely free cross-border travels." Starting from December 2003, they waged a sit-in protest for 83 days at the Centennial Hall of Korean Christianity (Hanguk gyohoe 100-junyeon ginyeom hoegwan) and led the subsequent amendment of the Law. Prior to that, they also participated in the campaign to legalize undocumented Chinese-Korean workers and won concessions from the government to give grace periods for leaving the country, or to extend the stay, for those who reported their visa status voluntarily.[8] However, the Alliance and the church ran into conflicts as the Alliance members demanded, for example, that the enforcement decree spelled out more concretely measures to implement the institutional improvements passed in the amendment of the Law. In the process, the Alliance left the church in 2005.

After leaving the church, the Alliance refurbished an old building that had been used as a *gosiwon*[!] to operate Urijip ("Our House"), a shelter for Joseonjok. The shelter is used by Joseonjok as a temporary residence while they settle in South Korea.[9] Many use the shelter when the whereabouts of their contacts in Korea are unclear, when they are looking for a job, or when they have to wait two or three months before the government alien registration card is issued. It is also used by many live-in housemaids who need housing only on weekends, by those who work as caregivers for the sick, and by men who work as day laborers.

The Alliance has approximately eight hundred members as of

8 The result was the Comprehensive Plan for Preventing Illegal Immigration (Bulbeob cheryuja jonghap bangji daechaek) (March 12, 2002) that was announced by the government.

! *Gosiwon*: A single-occupancy rooming facility traditionally rented by individuals preparing to take an examination (*gosi*) for a career in government. A room in a *gosiwon* is still synonymous with "cheap housing" –Tr.

9 Other organizations, such as the Federation of Overseas Koreans in South Korea, Joseonjok Church, and Jungguk Dongpo Town Sinmunsa, a newspaper company, also operate shelters.

July 2011, and its operating budget comes from membership fees and the finance businesses it operates.[10] The Alliance survived its separation from the church because of its strict rules and core activities. The Alliance organizes activities under five division headings: Organization, Living, Business, Mutual Aid Credit, and Culture and Publicity. Among these, the divisions on Living and Mutual Aid Credit are unique in what they do. The Living Division organizes volunteers to give concrete help on day-to-day living to its members; they care for children when they are sick, and they mend clothes for the members, for example. It is possible to operate such a program because there is a family-like atmosphere among members who want to realize the "Korean dream" as quickly as possible by helping one another. The Mutual Aid Credit program was established in 2006 and it connects members who can lend with those who need money. By 2010, five years after the program started, the total amount of money available for credit has reached over one billion (1,000,000,000,000) won. Judging from this amount, one can conclude that the membership's faith in the Alliance, and the organization's credibility among its members, have served as a foundation for strong membership unity and organizational autonomy.

The Alliance was able to separate itself from the church and firmly established itself as a self-representing organization advocating for its members' rights and interests as Joseonjok, primarily because it provides practical support for the day-to-day living of its members who experience economic hardships. As the chronicle of the Joseonjok migration to South Korea lengthens, the community is witnessing diversification of class. In the background, the Alliance articulates its mission as follows: "An organ-

10 Members pay 10,000 won per month, and only members can use the shelter. Anyone who is part of a "pyramid scheme," is a disciple of Falun Gong, or gambles, is disqualified from becoming a member. There are no other membership limitations, geographical or age-wise. However, many members have forfeited their membership rights because of the strict enforcement the rules, based on an interview with the president of the Alliance, July 4, 2011.

ization's reason for having started with listening to the voices of the weak." Their goal is to provide a stable residential environment through the shelter, for the Joseonjok in South Korea who need help to realize their dreams. Those who use the shelter, in turn, deposit their money with the Mutual Aid Credit Division, which helps new arrivals who are in need of help. The Alliance is still calling for a "guarantee of completely free cross-border travelling," and they demand that the South Korean government issue the F-4 visa—the permanent resident visa issued to other overseas Koreans who live in South Korea—to all Joseonjok in South Korea. A member of the Alliance defines its activities as follows:

> Some people say, let the church [handle] Joseonjok issues but...Never! History is always made by people themselves. Joseonjok history is written by Joseonjok. Others can help on the side, hold hands, and what not. [...] It's not that we Koreans from China are beggars who came here, is it? We don't go to places to beg. We're independent and we help each other, we shall push forward. (Interview with V, July 4, 2011)

(2) Young Generation's Communication Network

Many of the young Josenjok in South Korea are students. There are many who work in South Korea on an H2 (guest worker) visa or C3 (technology education) visa, but these workers lack political leadership and time (due to the fact that they work long hours) to form a community organization. In contrast, KCN is an organization that has been formed under a relatively liberal environment by students who use their student status to advocate rights and interests of Joseonjok.[11]

KCN was launched in December 2003 by master's and doctoral degree Joseonjok students in Korea with the purpose of pro-

---

11 Jaehan Jungguk yuhaksaeng yeonhaphoe (Chinese Foreign Students Association in South Korea) is an organization of mostly Han-Chinese students. It and KCN, the Joseonjok student network, are both registered with the Chinese Embassy in South Korea. A KCN member stated that while KCN had registered with the Embassy out of a fear that they might run into trouble when they become politically vocal in South Korea, their activities are not controlled or censored by the Embassy.

moting "friendship and exchange among Joseonjok foreign students, national development, and advancement of Korea-China friendship." There are estimated to be 5,000 members, and the number now includes undergraduate Joseonjok students. Since 2008, F-4 visas have been issued to Joseonjok students in Korea, and thus it has become difficult to identify the exact number of the Joseonjok students.

At the time that KCN was organized, Chinese-Korean immigration issues began to be discussed as a social problem, and the group began somewhat naively, and with an elitist perspective, believing that they could "re-engineer the Joseonjok image in South Korea." The public was bombarded with news of illegal Joseonjok immigrants, and KCN vowed to "1) improve the Joseonjok community image; 2) exchange information and build a network among Joseonjok students in Korea; and 3) play the role of a liaison for China-Korea friendship and economic and cultural exchanges."

To improve the image of the Chinese-Korean community, the students engaged themselves in volunteer activities, and they also regularly held academic seminars and workshops. Through these activities, they wanted to convey the message that not all Joseonjok are undocumented workers and that there are "students who came here to study." In order to change the biased perspective on the Chinese-Korean community, they exchanged information with Chinese-Korean organizations in Korea, bringing attention to the larger Joseonjok community. Thus cooperating with community organizations, the students shaped an agenda to better advocate for Joseonjok rights and interests.[12]

12 For example, the students carried out a variety of activities in alliance with the newspaper, *(Jungguk) Dongpo Taun Sinmun*, which was also founded in 2003. The students who founded KCN were living in Garibong, where the newspaper had its office, and it was quite easy for the students to align themselves with the paper, which was not religiously affiliated. One can say that this is a form of solidarity based on inter-local networking.

KCN, which gave its priority to political activities to secure rights of the Chinese-Korean in Korea, declared a change of direction in 2010. The students declared that they will now give priority to their status as students. In other words, as "foreign students," they would devote their efforts to their academic activities rather than to political activities that they, as an organization, were engaged in. They are currently focusing their efforts on three programs only: the seminar series; presentation of master's and doctoral theses; and orientation for new students. They are keeping other activities to a minimum.

There are still unresolved government policy issues concerning the status of Chinese-Korean workers, such as the guest worker program and the technology-training program. However, the students are intentionally distancing themselves from any issues involving political struggles and implications. That is because the advocacy role the students played earlier has been taken up by various Chinese-Korean news media. Because of widespread Internet access, newspapers published by the Chinese-Korean community reflect the voices of the community with little time lag, and other community organizations have now become mature enough to carry out activities on their own. Thus, KCN has concluded that its role now is to engage in and to receive recognition from South Korean society by focusing their efforts on academic work.

2) The Chinese-Korean Community: Community-building and Conflicts

As we have seen, the development of the media played a pivotal role in taking the KCN students "back" to their "duty" as students. The Chinese-Korean media plays an important role in exchanging and communicating information, and in providing critique of the government's policies. The Chinese-Korean media as a whole has been growing rapidly since the 2000s due to the rapid spread of Internet services. Major newspapers in the Chinese-Korean community include *Dongbuga Sinmun* (Northeast Asia Newspaper), *Jungguk Dongpo Taun Sinmun* (Chinese-Korean Town Newspaper), *Hanjung Beomnyul Sinmun* (Korea-China Legal Newspaper), *Hanjung Sangbo* (Korea-China Commercial Bulletin), and *Heungnyonggang Sinmun* (Heilongjian Newspaper) (MUN Min, 2010: 77). Of these, the *Jungguk Dongpo Taun Sinmun*, or simply *Dongpo Taun Sinmun (DTS)* is the leading newspaper providing a communication channel for the community. Furthermore, the newspaper has been leading efforts to create a Jungguk Dongpo Town in the Guro-Garibong area. I will now focus on describing the development of and strategies behind this effort.

The idea of building a "town" initially came from KIM Yong-pil, a reporter and editor-in-chief of *DTS*. He wanted to build, in Daerim-dong, a Jungguk Dongpo Town Center as a local networking hub. In order to engage with Korean society at large, he felt it was important to specialize the Guro-Daerim-Garibong area, since it had the largest population concentration of Chinese-Koreans. The name of the newspaper reflects his conviction. It is *Dongpo* Taun *Sinmun*, not just *Dongpo Sinmun*. He wanted to provide diversed information to the Chinese-Korean community and to actively engage Korean society at the same time; he envisioned a specialized local community.

Founded in 2003, *DTS* was distributed free of charge and carried a variety of information. From business operational perspective, free circulation is burdensome, but the demand for the paper was explosive. The paper has been in operation for eight years now, and it plays a major role of communication within the Chinese-Korean community. However, on the question of whether or not it actually created a Dongpo Town, a "town" that has built *the* Chinese-Korean Community in the Guro area and actively engages Korean society in it, with media as its intermediary, the answer is skeptical. In the Guro-Garibong area, it is easy enough to come in contact with various aspects of Joseon-jok community life, and a variety of information is available there. However, the Chinese-Koreans themselves believe that the area is gradually becoming isolated from Korean society, rather than furthering engaging with it.

Given that the area is a home to many Chinese-Korean organizations, small groups, and newspapers mentioned above, why are they unable to develop common activities in the name of a community "town"? One reason is that not all organizations and groups within the community cooperate with each other. Organizations with similar goals and functions come together and fall apart. These are telling signs of disunion within the community. What are some of the differences between these organizations in terms of their activities?

The Federation of Repatriating Overseas Koreans was launched in 2005. It is a meeting of Chinese-Koreans who have repatriated to Korea. As such, the organization helps those who want to be naturalized and settle down in South Korea; they provide education for naturalization; and they operate a center for supporting Chinese-Koreans to stay in South Korea. A similar organization, the Alliance of Returning Overseas Koreans (Gwiguk dongpo yeonhaphoe), was founded in 2008 and began their activities. Their official name is the Geumcheon-gu Alliance of Returning Overseas Koreans, and officially it is an organization of "overseas Koreans from any nation who is returning to South Korea for the purpose of recovering nationality, permanent residence, and is now living in Geumcheon-gu." It says overseas Koreans from *any* nation, but in reality, its membership is for Chinese-Koreans, and although the organization takes the form of an "alliance," it operates more like a social club. This organization, unable to show much difference in its activities with the Federation above, formed, with a few other Chinese-Korean organizations, the Federation of Overseas Koreans in South Korea in August of the same year. Member organizations in the latter Federation include the above-mentioned Alliance of Returning Overseas Koreans, Hometown Social Club (Donghyang chinmokhoe), and Chinese-Korean Merchants Association (Jungguk dongpo sangin yeonhaphoe). However, this latter federation does not include the Federation of Repatriating Overseas Koreans, mentioned at the beginning of this paragraph.

Nor did the Federation of Overseas Koreans in South Korea form a union with the Joseonjok Alliance. Looking at their names only, there is little difference between the two organizations. Why were they unable to form a federation together? The two organizations have different geographical and class bases in South Korea. The Joseonjok Alliance serves the Chinese-Korean community across the country with their base in Hongje-dong, Seodaemun-gu. In contrast, the Federation serves the Chinese-Korean population mostly in the Garibong area of Geumcheon-gu. In addition, in terms of class difference, the Alliance serves the relatively poorer population, while the Federation is mostly run by merchants or small-business owners. These differences make solidarity between these two organizations difficult.

> The [various Chinese-Korean] organizations have different perspectives on what we should be doing in South Korea. [...] Initially, everybody came here to make money, to make a living. Generally speaking, they were not young people. They came here for only one reason: to feed their children and give them a good life. From the Alliance's point of view, we think people come here, not thinking about how they are going to make it here and be successful in Korea, but thinking about how they could make it in China, be successful there, and to take root there. People fuss about letting us have the *dongpo* (F4) visa, but I don't think we should voluntarily give up the Manchurian land—the land that the Joseonjok in China developed—and the efforts we put there. So, people think differently about our children and our children's children living and making it in China. That is the difference we have with other organizations. (Joseonjok Alliance, July 4, 2011)

Despite of large opinion gaps among Joseonjok community groups in Korea, efforts continued until quite recently to form a united federation. Discord among Chinese-Korean groups not only gives a bad image to Chinese-Koreans themselves but to the public at large in Korea. Thus the community groups want to come together to better advocate for Chinese-Korean rights and interests, and to shape the cultural discourse of the community. However, their wish will be hard to fulfill in reality.

5. Exchanges between Chinese-Korean and Korean Society

1) Communication Gap at Workplaces

Most Chinese-Koreans working as laborers are middle-aged or older. One characteristic distinct in their job history is the high turn-over rate. This is true regardless of gender. At first when they arrive in Korea, they start with any job they can find. Once they become part of the local network of Chinese-Koreans, they change jobs in search for better conditions. In the case of men, they work most commonly at construction jobs. In the case of women, they first start working at motels or restaurants; as they become settled, they move on to work as live-in housemaids or caregivers for the sick, and receive relatively higher wages.

Men who work as day laborers on construction jobs want to find more stable work in a company or a corporation. Some in the construction field work as electrical or electronics specialists; the pride of these men in their work is very high. They believe that they are recognized at their workplaces because they are more educated, and cultivated, and skilled than Korean day laborers. In the case of women, they also have much pride in their work. Some of them have relayed stories of having received an expensive gift from their employer while working as a live-in housemaid or caregivers for the sick. In comparison to work in other fields, theses positions bring with them unusually better chances of communication with Korean employers; accordingly, the degree of mutual trust is high in this job category.

Chinese-Koreans feel that they are recognized as skilled workers in South Korea. The reason for their high job turn-over rate has only partly to do with wages, and it is usually not the decisive factor. They quit their work when they feel they are humiliated and discriminated and when they can no longer sustain their dreams about their life and future in Korea. This indicates, on one hand, that they do have job choices. On the other hand, it confirms that discrimination is the most difficult aspect of living in Korea for them.

Workplace discrimination is generally less rampant now than before, but general disregard and discrimination against Chinese-Koreans are still serious. What is the cause of this discrimination, in the minds of the Chinese-Koreans themselves? The Chinese-Koreans interviewed for this study did not think that all Koreans discriminate against them but that the level of discrimination varies depending on the educational level and the profession of Koreans.

> Going to the workplace, too, these Koreans, they are big fish in a small pond... One tries to have a conversation with them, and you know, they are day laborers, not company workers. Things can get pretty low. So one tries to have a conversation, and they would say things like "You have apples in China?" Or, they ask if we have this or that. These questions are really frustrating. They ask, "do you have this where you come from?" And we think to ourselves, "We have even better things to eat in China." (Interview with C, July 27, 2011)

Most of the Joseonjok in Korea work in 3D jobs, but they come from diverse job backgrounds in China. As we can see from <Table 1>, they all received a similar level of education and enjoyed a similar level of living standards under the socialist system in China. They also held various occupations, working as civil servants, bank clerks, or store clerks. However, in Korea, they all commonly work in 3D occupations, meeting Koreans who are less educated than they are, and who have lived a harsher life than they have. And they are disregarded and discriminated against by these Koreans. Chinese-Koreans in Korea say that the most painful part about living in Korea is not the hard work they do but the discrimination that comes out of people's ignorance.

> The owners lecture at you full of spite and they look down at you. That's what's most difficult. [...] They cast their eyes down on you and say "do this or do that before you finish." They don't even use the honorifics, and in many cases they end up using foul language at you. You are just a dog to them, and so when that happens, you work there for two or three hours, and then you take the apron off and walk out. (Interview with F, August 14, 2011)

Another form of discrimination that Chinese-Koreans experience in Korea is delays in wage payment. For those who have come to Korea to earn money, payment delay is one of the hardest pains to endure. The phenomenon is more serious in local areas than in Seoul, and it has been known that many employers would hire the same Chinese-Korean worker after delaying his or her wage payment. Chinese-Korean workers feel frustrated that nothing happens when they bring such cases to the attention of the Ministry of Employment and Labor. A few years ago, "A" filed a complaint with the Ministry of Employment and Labor to receive 900,000 won in back wages. However, in third-party arbitration he was told to "accept 500,000 won or lose your job with no payment at all." He agreed to the terms of arbitration. While they are frustrated, the workers are also puzzled by the South Korean system that allows factories to continue operating after workers are cheated out of their wages for a week or ten days.

Responses of Chinese-Korean workers to discrimination and disrespect against them vary according to personal disposition and age. When a conflict arises at the workplace, there are those who try communicate by initiating a gesture of reconciliation, and there are those who swallow the situation on his or her own and internally develop a disregard for Koreans. The older and more experienced Chinese-Koreans, such as "M," would take out the young Korean colleagues "to a restaurant, have food together, buy them *soju*, and make up." Then there are people like "L" who—after realizing that one is treated according to one's ability at work—does not pay any attention to trivial conflicts at the workplace.

However, reconciliatory gestures are possible only when one feels that the other party is at least someone who is open to communication. Such a gesture would be the best way to build relationships and make friends in South Korea, but in most cases the worker chooses to take the conflict personally and to mentally ignore Koreans. A conflict arose with a Korean colleague where "C" was working. The Korean suddenly said "You are all *gyopo* (overseas Koreans), aren't you? You are all illegal, right? Bring your IDs!" 'C' said he would just smile, telling himself, "You are uneducated, or you don't know the times we are living in." He does not try to talk any more with such people because he feels it is not worth the effort. Thus there is a double strategy in their efforts to be recognized by Koreans: they ignore Koreans who do not recognize them, and they accept the ignorance of Koreans.

Again, what do Chinese-Korean workers think about how Koreans disregard and discriminate against Chinese-Koreans, treating them as "lower than an animal" or "as a dog?" The Chinese-Koreans interviewed do not think that the Korean population as a whole is pre-disposed this way, or that even individuals are pre-disposed this way. They attribute the cause of the discrimination and disrespect to the experience of the individual's socio-economic hardship and the resulting lack of educational opportunity, on the one hand, and to particular socio-structural features of capitalism.

> If we get into an argument, for example, they would just raise their voice without reason. They raise their voice to overpower the other, not discerning what is right or wrong. And when you see them in a gathering place ... they don't know how to be considerate of others. They are just busy looking after their own interest. That is because they grew up in a capitalist country where you have to dominate the other to survive, right? I think that is the primary reason. (Interview with F, August 14, 2011)

According to the testimonies of these workers, it seems that—except in some cases of live—in housework or caregivers, in which cases Koreans receive direct care from the workers—not much workplace communication is taking place between Chinese-Koreans and Koreans. Except for a few, most of the Chinese-Koreans interviewed for this study did not have Korean friends, and more than anything else they were distrustful of Koreans. They said that when a problem occurs, whether it is at home or at work, Koreans become suspicious of them and they exclude them and keep distance from them; that is why they say they have trained themselves to not open themselves to Koreans. Thus, many Chinese-Koreans have closed their minds off to individual Koreans. However, at group or collective level of the community, there are efforts to communicate with South Korean society at large.

2) The Politics of Difference in Chinese-Korean Community

The Chinese-Korean population center of the Guro-Garibong-Daerim area does not have a single unified federation that represents the Chinese-Korean community as a whole, at either the local or national level. However, there are many organizations and small groups in the area that engage in dialogue with Korean society in various ways. In the case of the Joseonjok Alliance, whose officers emphasize the importance of historical consciousness, they said, "[we] do not have to be in solidarity with one another simply because we are also Chinese-Korean. If there is a common point of view, we can be in solidarity and engage in exchanges with any organization in Korea." Thus, the Alliance has been in solidarity with Korean International Network (KIN) —an organization working with various Korean diaspora groups and their respective issues—since 2001when the Alliance participated in the campaign to revise the Law on Overseas Koreans. The two organizations have been in solidarity for over ten years now, and the Alliance participated again in the 2008 Campaign to Save Utoro and the 2009 Campaign to Save Sakhalin, both of which were led by KIN.

Many of the issues that Joseonjok face in Korea are related to labor and human rights issues. Thus whenever a political issue arises, the Alliance forms solidarity with labor organizations in Korea on a case-by-case basis.

The Federation of Overseas Koreans in South Korea, mentioned above, is engaged in solidarity activities with Korean organizations that are quite different from those with whom the Alliance works. Close to seventy-two percent of the Federation membership have Korean citizenship, and "because [we] should not be separated like water and oil as we live in Korea" the organization aims to promote cultural and arts exchanges first. Thus in 2010, the organization cooperated with the Federation of Artistic and Cultural Organizations of Korea (Hanguk munhwa yesul chong hyeophoe, or "Yechong" in short) and held a charity event to donate rice to the needy. Also, seeing ethnic Chinese in Korea represent China in a municipal festival of ASEAN migrants in Incheon, the Chinese-Korean Federation demanded a booth of their own and promoted Chinese-Korean dishes such as rice dumplings, corn noodle, and sweet rice *sundae*. The participation in the festival led to a series of articles in a local newspaper about Chinese-Koreans living in Korea. From the Federation's perspective, the readership of a local newspaper in Incheon is not limited to Chinese-Koreans but includes the general public in Korea; in this regard a series of articles about

Chinese-Koreans in such a newspaper was perceived as a way of raising the general population's understanding of their community.

The Federation also has a history education program. It holds history education seminars in cooperation with the National Secretariat of Cheondogyo, "the religion of Heavenly Way." The Federation also goes wherever it feels it can help people become aware of the presence of Chinese-Koreans in Korea. In this vein, it has participated in the Campaign to Save the Andong Traditional Market. Thus the Federation is active in participating in cultural events and not in political issues, because the "members who have acquired Korean citizenship must live in Korea as Koreans in the years ahead, and they must be assimilated, and they must know Korea."

Exchanges between Chinese-Korean communities and Korean society at large also take place outside of these organizational frameworks and at the level of everyday culture and activities as individuals make their presence known as Chinese-Koreans. The Federation of Repatriating (*gwihwan*) Overseas Koreans organizes volunteer street-cleaning in Daerim-dong; the volunteers are mostly elderly Chinese-Koreans. It is one of the efforts to change the larger public's image of Chinese-Koreans. The Chinese-Korean One Mind Association (Jungguk dongpo hanmaeum hyeophoe) operates the Corps of Hanmaeum Volunteers to help the needy in local neighborhoods. The volunteers participated in a national volunteer drive to help the residents in the Taean County on the west coast of Korea in the aftermath of the 2007 oil spill disaster. They also continue to sponsor meals for underprivileged children in elementary schools in the Daerim-dong area.

The Hanmaeum Association members also organized crime prevention volunteer groups and took responsibility for neighborhood patrol for public safety and crime prevention in cooperation with police. The volunteer crime prevention groups were organized to prevent the spread and reproduction of negative images about Chinese-Koreans, and to prevent their social standing from being reduced to the negative gaze of the general public, and to secure their legitimacy in Korean society. On the other hand, from the police perspective it may have made more sense to have the local Chinese-Korean community, a community of both the underprivileged and extraterritorial citizens who are not under their direct control, patrol the area. This police perspective may have found a match in the Chinese-Korean community's own desire to volunteer to "make Jungguk Dongpo Town a place of harmony and co-existence and to make it a safe and nice neighborhood to live." Thus there was an aspect in which the local Chinese-Korean community was mobilized in police propaganda, but clearly the voluntary activities were also efforts to re-engineer the community image through a compromise with Korean society at large.

Chinese-Korean residents in the Guro-Daerim-Garibong area have a strong tendency to live within the boundary of their local community; however, underneath the surface, they are seeking various ways to politically and culturally engage with Korean society. Engagement and exchanges with Korean society are possible as a community, through organizations or groups, not as individuals. Individual efforts have met with limitations, but when their opportunities for communication are joined by the goal of the community, communication possibilities open up.

6. Concluding Remarks

Charles Taylor uses the notion of the "politics of difference" in order to explain a community in terms of multiculturalism. In communitarianism, the politics of difference emphasize the importance of recognizing the unique identities of and the difference among individuals and groups who have been forced to assimilate with a majority identity; it also emphasizes the importance of "cultural survival." In the case of Nancy Fraser, she starts by asking, whose interests are counted as justice in an era of globalization? Are they the interests of the citizens of certain territorial boundaries, of the humanity at large on earth, or of the transnational crisis communities? She argues that a new, three-dimensional "framework" of justice should integrate economic redistribution, cultural recognition, and political representation (Nancy Fraser, 2010: 16-36).

Looking at Joseonjok in Korea from these perspectives, the individual and collective efforts of Joseonjok to form a singular community of their own, to communicate among themselves, and to resolve conflicts with South Korean society, ultimately, can be interpreted as a manifestation of the politics of difference, and as a frame for cultural recognition. Or, in Habermasian language, one could say that their efforts constitute reproduction and re-structuring processes in the public sphere through the agents' communication. The Joseonjok who now enter South Korea legally, after the amendment of the Law, are changing their communities and cultures from within, and they engage and exchange with Korean society from both within and without its borders. It seems that the Chinese-Korean community, as a whole, is poised to enter a new stage of communication.

The Joseonjok from China move to South Korea with a sense of honor and pride in the country of their ancestors, their motherland. However, as they experience discrimination, disregard, conflict, and disappointment, South Korea degenerates into a place where they put their cultural resources to make economic gains and leave; it ceases to be a place to settle down. In other words, in the globalizing world of neo-liberalism, Chinese-Koreans, as a whole in South Korea, are treated as no more than a source of cheap labor, and in the process their adamant emphasis on the "national discourse" loses its footing. Not quite "foreign," and not quite "Korean," their status then becomes all the more ambiguous.

However, as I have examined thus far, when migrants—in this case, Chinese-Koreans—occupy a particular neighborhood and settle down in a country, regardless of how young or old such a settlement is, they, as a member of society at large in the new country, constantly exchange information, pick up practices of the new culture, and enter into conflicts as they try to engage themselves and the host society in communications and exchanges with each other. They see the differences, the products of mutually different socio-structural conditions, and they ponder about the relationship, about how to position each other and themselves.

Accordingly, in the current politics of discourse in South Korea, the question should not be "How is the Chinese-Korean multicultural?" Instead, local Chinese-Korean communities and Korean society should build a new public sphere together; not confine Chinese-Koreans within the framework of either the "multiculturalism discourse" or the "*dongpo* discourse;" and pay attention to new Chinese-Korean cultural formations. Chinese-Koreans and Koreans have a common ancestry. But today they live in two very separate worlds of everyday life and culture. Identifying the lines of various differences, and delineating them accurately and meticulously, would indeed be a critique of the exclusivist discourse of multiculturalism in South Korea. Such a critique would, at the same time, open possibilities for newly engaging with such a "Joseonjok community" in South Korea.

Bibliography

Charles Taylor (1994), *Multiculturalism*. Princeton University Press.

David Fitzgerald (2002), "Rethinking the 'Local' and 'Transnational.'" Annual meeting of the American Sociological Association, Chicago.

Gukje Goryeo Hakhoe Asea Bunhoe (Asia Chapter, International Society for Korean Studies) (1999), *Jungguk Joseonjok gongdongche yeongu* (A study on Chinese Joseonjok community), Yeonbyeon gyoyuk chulpansa (Yanbian Education Press).

HONG Se-yeong and KIM Geum-ja (2010), "Joseonjok ganbyeongin ui munhwa jeogeung gyeongheom e gwanhan yeongu: Noin ganbyeong seobiseu reul jegong haneun Joseonjok yeoseong eul jungsim euro" (A study on the cultural adaptation experience of Joseonjok Caregivers for the sick: With focus on Joseonjok women who provide care services to the elderly), *Hanguk nonyeonhak* (The Korean Gerontological Studies), Vol. 30, No. 4.

JEONG Gi-seon, translator (2011), *Hanguk imin jeongchaek ui ihae* (Understanding Korean immigration policy), Baeksan Seodang.

KIM Hyun-mi (2008), "Jungguk Joseonjok ui Yeonguk iju gyeongheom: Hanin taun geojuja ui sarye reul jungsim euro" (The Chinese Joseonjok experience of migration to England: With a focus on the case of a Koreatown resident) in *Hanguk munhwa illyuhak* (Korean Cultural Anthropology), Vol. 42, No. 2.

___________ (2009), "Bangmun chwieop jaejung dongpo ui il gyeongheom gwa saenghwal sege" (Chinese-Korean guest workers' work experience and their daily routine) in *Hanguk munhwa illyuhak* (Korean Cultural Anthropology), Vol. 42, No. 2.

KIM Yeong-gyeong (2008), "Hanguk nae Joseonjok cheongnyeon-deul ui sahoe munhwa jeogeungnyeok hyangsang eul wihan yogu bunseok" (A demand analysis on capacity improvement of socio-cultural adaptation by Joseonjok youth in South Korea) in *Hanguk gidokgyo sangdamhak hoeji* (Korean Christian Pastoral Counseling Bulletin), No. 15.

KWON Tae-hwan (2003), *Jungguk Joseonjok sahoe ui byeonhwa: 1990-nyeondae ihu reul jungsim euro* (Changes in Chinese Joseonjok society: With focus on the post-1990s era), The Institute for Social Development and Policy Research, Seoul National University.

Naensi Peureijeo (Nancy Fraser) (2010), *Jiguhwa sidae ui jeongui* (Justice in a globalizing world). Greenbee.

MUN Hyeong-jin (2008), "Hanguk nae Joseonjok nodongja deul ui galdeung sarye e gwanhan yeongu" (A study on conflict cases of Joseonjok workers in South Korea), *The International Area Review* (Gukje jiyeok yeongu), Vol. 12, No. 1.

MUN Min (2010), "Jaehan Jungguk dongpo danche hyeonhwang gwa gwaje" (The current status of Chinese-Korean organzations in South Korea and their challenges), *MIDRI REPORT*.

PARK U (2011), "Hanguk cheryu Joseonjok 'danche' ui byeonhwa wa injeong tujaeng e gwanhan yeongu" (A study on changes in Joseonjok "groups" in South Korea and their recognition struggle), *Economy & Society* (Gyeongje wa sahoe), No. 91.

Saskia Sassen (1998), *The Mobility of Labor and Capital*, Cambridge University Press.

SEOL Dong-hoon (1999), "Oegugin nodongja wa Hanguk sahoe ui sangho jagyong" (Interaction between foreign workers and Korean society), Nodong munje nonjip (Papers on Labor Issues), No. 13.

Stephen Castles & Alsatar Davidson (2000), *Citizenship and Mi-*

gration: Globalization and the Politics of Belonging, Palgrave.

Wireugen HABEOMAS (Jürgen Habermas) (2004), *Gongnonjang ui gujo byeondong* (The Structural Transformation of the Public Sphere). Nanam.

YE Dong-geun (2009), "Geulobal sidae Jungguk ui cheje jeonhwan gwa dosi jongjok gongdongche jaehyeongseong: Bug-gyeong wangjing koria taun ui Joseonjok gongdongche sarye yeongu" (Chinese system change in an age of globalization and reconfiguration of urban ethnic community: A case study of Joseonjok community in the Wangjing Koreatown in Beijing), *Minjok Yeongu* (ethnic research), Vol. 43, 159-185.

YI Chun-bok (2010), *Paran gwa gokjeol geurigo himang* (Disturbances, vicissitudes, and hope). Doseo Chulpan Gyeong-jin.

YI Jin-yeong (1999), "Jungguk sosu minjok jeongchaek ui ironjeok gicho e gwanhayeo" (On the theoretical foundation of the Chinese policy on ethnicity), *Journal of Asia Pacific Studies* (Atae yeongu), Vol. 6, No. 2.

YI Jin-yeong and PARK U (2009), "Jaehan Jungguk Joseonjok nodongja jipdan ui hyeongseong gwajeong e gwanhan yeongu" (A study on the formation of the Chinese-Korean worker population in South Korea), *Hanguk dongbuga nonchong* (Korea North East Asia Papers), Vol. 51.

YI Mi-ae (2008), *Garibong-dong Jungguk geori e seo ui Joseonjok yeoseong ui wichiseong e daehan munhwa jirijeok yeongu* (A cultural geographical study of Joseonjok women's positionality in the Garibong-dong China street). Master's thesis, Cutural Studies Department, Chung-Ang University.

YI Seung-ryul (2007), *Dongbuga sidae wa Joseonjok* (The era of Northeast Asia and Joseonjok). Bagyeongsa.

YIM Gye-sun (2003), *Uri ege daga on Joseonjok eun nugu inga* (Who are the Joseonjeok who came to us)? Hyeonamsa.

YIM Seon-il (2010), Esnisiti byeonhyeong eul tonghan Hanguk sahoe iju nodongja ui munhwa byeonyong yeongu (A study on migrant workers' cultural transformation through ethnicity change in South Korea). Ph.D. Dissertation, Sociology Department, SongKongHoe University.
YUN In-jin (2004), *Korian diaseupora* (Korean Diaspora). Korea University Press.

A Study on the Settlement Experience and Everyday Life of North Korean Arrivals in South Korea

by KIM Sung-kyung

Humanities Korea Research Professor

Institute for East Asian Studies at SungKongHoe University

1. Introduction

The total number of North Koreans arriving in South Korea from 1953 until 1989 was six hundred seven. This number has continually increased, and since 2001, about one thousand North Koreans have been arriving in the South annually. As of April 2011, the total aggregate number of North Koreans living in South Korea has reached approximately twenty-one thousand. Considering that the estimated number of North Koreans currently staying in China is thirty-five thousand (YOON In-jin, 2009, 27), their number in South Korea is certain to continue to increase in the future. During the Cold War era, North Koreans defecting to the South were hailed as "brave soldiers of surrender" (*gwisun yongsa*), and as heroes symbolizing an ideological victory on the part of South Korea. However, since North Koreans began breaking away from North Korea in large numbers beginning in the late 1990s, they have been occupying multiple positions in South Korea as the "economically underprivileged" who need welfare state support and, at the same time, as a symbol of Cold War ideology that still runs through both South and North Korea. On the other hand, from the human rights perspective, their predicament cannot be resolved at the level of a single country, as they move to China and often traverse through many other countries in Asia. Furthermore, the "migration industry," which makes the mass migration of North Koreans possible, is a hotbed of human trafficking, labor exploitation, and human rights violations. In most cases, North Koreans initially cross the border to China and remain there illegally for a mid-to long-term period; they then go through other countries in Asia before finally arriving in South Korea. During the course of their movement, numerous illegal transactions and activities take place and the positions of neighboring countries in how they deal with the migrants are often sharply different. Additionally, due to the residual Cold War ideology, it is difficult to define the status of theses North Koreans. In light of these factors taken all together, the North Korean arrival issue is unique, and the North Korean arrivals, as a group, are incomparable to any other migration group that has been the subject of a migration study thus far. The migration by North Koreans who defect from North Korea is a paradoxical articulation of the North-South Korea division, a Cold War remnant, on the one hand, and the world-wide phenomenon of migration that corroborates globalization in action, on the other; thus the task of finding and systematizing an appropriate theory and methodology to analyze the North Korean migration is all the more complex. Thus, this chapter seeks to establish a theoretical and methodological framework for studying the North Korean migration phenomenon. I introduce major trends in migration studies and critically discuss their implications to theoretically and methodologically contextualize the particularities of the phenomenon. Also, I examine the settlement process of North Korean arrivals in South Korea at the level of their everyday activities; applying the thick description methodology used in anthropology, I examine how they understand, accept, and resist or negotiate with South Korean social structure in their new environment.

2. Contextual Framework for Researching North Korean Arrivals

Migration studies in the West may be generally categorized under three paradigms. The first is the demographic explanation paradigm; the second is the assimilation paradigm; and the third is the multiculturalism paradigm. The first paradigm recognizes migration as a social phenomenon that occurs as a result of need and demand. Schematically put, it explains that migration takes places from poor countries in the south, which have a population surplus, to rich countries in the north, which have a labor-force shortage. The assimilation paradigm has been useful in explaining the relationship between ethnic minorities and the ethnic (or racial) majority of the places where the minority groups settle. The third is the paradigm that takes a multiculturalism approach to migration study. The multiculturalism approach to migration studies appeared at a time when concerns about racism deepened in the United States, a nation of immigrants. As such, these studies raise issues about inequalities faced by different immigration groups due to their cultural, ethnic, and racial differences; they recognize the differences among various immigration groups, and between immigrant and settler groups; and they emphasize the importance of the co-existence of multiple cultures and races.

When using these paradigms as an analytical tool, they should be modified according to the situation and particular attributes of the migrants and their country of settlement (or origin), and applied selectively. Moreover, with the migration phenomenon becoming more complex, one now frequently finds that multiple paradigms are used simultaneously. For example, in the case North Korean defectors, their migration and settlement issues can be analyzed within the assimilation paradigm framework, but the phenomenon can also be explained in terms of demographics. That is to say, in the 1990s, after reform and liberalization policies in China began in earnest, the ethnic Korean population in three northeastern provinces in China decreased, and it became relatively easier for North Koreans to cross the border with China. Thus, the decrease of the ethnic Korean population in China can be seen as a major factor in the increase of North Korean arrivals in China. However it is difficult to empirically prove a correlation between these two variables. Furthermore, most North Korean arrivals in China stay there for a mid-to long-term period, using China only as a passageway to migrate to either South Korea or another country; thus, the demographics paradigm has limitations in explaining certain aspects that are unique to the North Korean migration phenomenon.

When the assimilation paradigm is applied to the study of the North Korean arrivals in South Korea, one must consider a number of local particularities. While it is evident that North Koreans are viewed as a minority group that should be assimilated into South Korean society, it is also true that there are apparatuses working to separate North Koreans from even other migrant groups in South Korea. Deeply rooted Cold War ideology in South Korea distinguishes North Koreans from other migration groups, at times culturally, and at other times institutionally. The nationalist perspective that emphasizes the "compatriot" (*dongpo*) status of North Koreans often operates in a repressive mode of not accepting cultural and linguistic differences between North and South Koreans. In other words, the nationalist logic is that North Koreans are not "foreigners" like other migrants in Korea and thus must be assimilated into South Korean society. At the same time, because they are from North Korea, which is in direct confrontation with South Korea, North Koreans are often more alienated than the other "aliens" in South Korea. This ambiguous position of the North Korean arrivals in South Korea may shed much light on the multiculturalism paradigm. In other words, North Koreans are not a separate biological race. However, there has to be an empirical study on whether or not the Cold War ideology—deeply ingrained in the political and cultural life of Korea—has made North Koreans a separate social "race."

Another difficulty facing the study of North Korean arrivals in South Korea is the question of how to define the research subjects. Those who argue that they should be defined as economic or environmental refugees and that neighboring countries should respect their refugee status and protect their human rights point out political repression in North Korea; or in the case of those who face deportation by Chinese authorities, they argue that the deportees will be treated harshly if they are sent back and that therefore they should be given refugee status in China to protect their human rights, as well as those of other North Koreans in similar situation in China (JEONG Ju-sin, 2009, 177-186; YI Yong-ho, 2002; YI Geum-sun and YUN Yeo-sang, 2006; IM Chae-wan and CHOE Yeong-gwan, 2000). On the other hand, there are those who argue that most of the North Korean arrivals do not qualify as refugees according to international law. A refugee as defined by the leading international refugee convention and protocol is someone who leaves his or her country because of political persecution.[1] In the case of North Koreans who

1 According to Article 1 of the Convention Relating to the Status of Refugees "the term 'refugee' shall apply to any person who" [...] "owing to well-founded fear of being persecuted for reasons of race, religion, nationality, membership of a particular social group or political opinion, is outside the country of his nationality and is unable or, owing to such fear, is unwilling to avail himself of the protection of that country; or who, not having a nationality and being outside the country of his former habitual residence as a result of such events, is unable or, owing to such fear, is unwilling to return to it." (UNHCR, 1997, 12) [This English text has been quoted from the following source: http://www.unhcr.org/3b66c2aa10.html, April 8, 2012. -Tr.]

have defected, most of them have done so to go to China or South Korea for economic reasons, not because of political persecution. Furthermore, it has been pointed out that after the introduction of markets in North Korea, North Koreans began having broader experiences of everyday life through formal and informal trade activities across the Chinese border; it has been suggested that this experience, and their admiration of South Korean culture, are the major push factors behind the more recent phenomenon of North Korean defections. Accordingly, scholars recently have put forth the argument that North Koreans who defect from their country should be defined as "economic migrants" (AHN Jong-su, 2010; NOH Gwi-nam, 2011; YUN In-jin, 2009). They point out that while it is true that these North Koreans leave North Korea in order to avoid a food crisis, which is an environmental disaster, they increasingly escape for other reasons. Such reasons include wanting to have a "better future," "higher quality of life through self development," and "better educational environment," as well as a "vague adoration for South Korea based on their contact with South Korean popular culture" (KIM In-seong, 2005; interview with "C" in 2011; interview with "K" in 2011). Thus, it is argued that it makes more sense to see these North Koreans as economic migrants. However, this single-framework approach of analyzing North Korean arrivals as either refugees or economic migrants also has limitations in that it cannot adequately contextualize the layered meaning of *talbuk*, or "defecting from North Korea." Even if one concedes that many of these North Koreans illegally cross the border to China for economic reasons, every step of their migration path is mired in extreme danger due to the particular condition of North and South Korean confrontation and the Chinese policy of forced deportation; from a human rights perspective, the illegal status of their migration presents a strong case for granting them refugee status. In terms of their status in South Korea, they are, as a group, the recipient of welfare state protection and at the same time a source of potential threat, further complicating attempts to characterize and define their *talbuk*, or "defector" status.

Recent studies on North Korean arrivals have increased sharply in Korea, but their theoretical/methodological framework is still weak. Most of these studies can be grouped under three general categories of identifying the present state of North Korean arrivals: studying the emotional difficulties that the North Korean arrivals experience and ways to address them from a psychological perspective; studying the adaptation process of North Korean arrivals; and examining policy issues. While there are differences in terms of degree, these existing studies rely mostly on the assimilation paradigm and do not give enough contextualization of the particular conditions of North and South Korea. Examples of these studies include: a study on the reality of North Korean arrivals by a religious organization (Joeun Beot deul (Good Friends), 1999); analyses of the psychological trauma of North Korean arrivals (JEON U-taek *et al*, 2010; EOM Tae-wan, 2010); studies on the settlement issues of North Korean arrivals in South Korea (JEONG Ju-sin, 2005; GWAK Hae-ryong, 2005); studies on the problems that the North Korean adolescents face in adapting to South Korean society (PARK Yun-suk and YUN In-jin, 2007; KIM Yun-yeong, 2005); and a study on the economic independence of North Korean women arrivals (JANG Myeong-seon and YI Ae-ran, 2010). Most of these studies are either skewed in that they focus too much on "identifying the actual situation" of the somewhat unique North Korean migration phenomenon, or they focus only on how the North Korean arrivals could successfully settle in South Korea. Thus these studies are lacking in theoretical rumination on "how" the North Korean arrivals themselves become assimilated in or excluded from South Korean society, and how their culture, experience, language, and values are altered and reconfigured in the process of their migration and settlement. These studies therefore tacitly define a human subject as a passive being that adapts to a social structure; the studies are thus limited in explaining the dynamic interaction between agency and social structure.

Another problem is that most of these studies rely on quantitative research methods. Of course, accumulation of statistical data on the identities of North Korean arrivals and on the level of their adaptation to South Korean society can be meaningful in itself. However, the quantitative methods artificially establish the scope of the research hypothesis and it is difficult for such methods to capture the multiplicity of the "meaning" of migration and of living in new society. In a study recently published, YI Hee-yeong (2010) applies an oral history method in analyzing social and political identities of North Korean arrivals in South Korea. This study is meaningful in that it critically reflects on the limitations of quantitative research methods and carries out an in-depth examination of the construction of the political identity of North Korean arrivals using a qualitative research method. However, this study explains the construction of identity as a process of interaction between an individual and the generalized Other, limiting the scope of the North Korean arrivals' identity construction to the micro-level only. Clearly, the micro-level relationship between the individual and the Other has a significant impact on identity construction, but this study overlooks the socio-structural conflicts experienced by North Koreans who arrive in South Korea, a foreign society to them. Thus, in this chapter I suggest that studies on the migration phenomenon of North Korean arrivals approach the subject from the perspective of structuration theory while applying anthropological methodologies to capture the relational dynamics between the structure and agent in the migration-settlement process of the North Korean arrivals.

3. Studying the Everyday Life of North Korean Arrivals: Structuration Theory and Anthropological Approach

Anthony Giddens explains how agency is either limited or enabled by structure, on the one hand, and how agency transforms the structure, on the other. The core of his structuration theory is the concept of the duality of structure, and its attempt to prove the relationship between structure and agency through this concept, moving away from the existing dualism in sociology that separates objectivism and subjectivism, and between structure and agency[2]. The concept of the duality of structure is as follows:

> According to the notion of the duality of structure, the structural properties of social systems are both medium and outcome of the practices they recursively organize. Structure is not "external" to individuals: as memory traces, and as instantiated in social practices, it is in a certain sense more "internal" than exterior to their activities in Durkheimian sense. Structure is not to be equated with constraint but is always both constraining and enabling.* (Giddens, 1998 [K], 74)

This notion of the duality of structure has certain advantages; it overcomes the presumption of the passivity of agency in social structural analyses; it also overcomes the limitations of analyses that focus only on agency actions, since their results are microscopic and subjective. In other words, this theory utilizes the analytical standards of both structure and agency at the same

2 Giddens' concept of the duality of structure has much similarity to that of Pierre Bourdieu's "structured structure" and "structuring structure" (Bourdieu, 1977). Bourdieu argues that the structured structure and structuring structure exist within *habitus*. In other words, habitus is the outcome of a social structure and the social structure itself at the same time. *Habitus* is constant but indicates a predisposition to a possibility of movement; that is to say, as a structured structure, it operates as a structure that structures actions and representations (Bourdieu, 1984, 170).

* This passage of Giddens' original text has been cited from the following: Anthony Giddens, *The Constitution of Society: Outline of the Theory of Structuration*, University of California Press, 1986, 25. The author has cited from the 1998 Korean version of this book, which is cited as Giddens, 1998 (K) –Tr.

time, and by focusing on the dialectical relationship between these two, it has the advantage of identifying how actors construct/re-construct everyday expereince.

According to Giddens, social structures are composed of "rules" and "resources." Rules include symbols (such as language) and norms, while resources are defined as ruling structures (political, economic, power, and authority apparatuses) (Giddens, 1998 [K], 78-86). In other words, by rules, Giddens means particular technologies or generalized customs that make social actions possible, and by resources he refers to a series of means that enable or constrain human actions. When an individual engages oneself in a social action the individual acts by endlessly applying, through one's capacity for knowledge, or "knowledgeability," rules and resources. Also, an agent's performance is carried out only with the rules and resources available to each agent within his or her social environment, and an agent may develop his or her capacity, which is structurally constructed, in creative and innovative ways that correspond to his or her new environment (Sewell 1992, 4-20). An agent may constantly monitor one's actions reflexively, and by assuming that others are monitoring his or her actions in a similar manner, the individual form "stocks of knowledge" and legitimize his or her own actions based on this.[3]

An agent recognizes the relationship between his action and structure, and performs and legitimizes an action based on this recognition. Such a process takes place at three different levels of consciousness. The first is the level of the unconscious seated in the depth of one's being, thus the motive for the action is not revealed at this level. The second is the level of the practical consciousness. At this level, the actor's motive or the institutional rules and resources are recognized and performed, but not ver-

3 Anthony Giddens borrowed the concept of "stocks of knowledge" from Alfred Schutz. He has also borrowed ethnomethodology from Erving Goffman and Harold Garfinkel as major concepts in social structuration theory.

bally enunciated. The last is the level of the discursive consciousness, and it refers to an explanation of knowledge and communication through discursive languages. The difference between practical consciousness and discursive consciousness is not clearly demarcated; rather, there exists only the difference between "what can be put into words" and "what has to be simply done" (Giddens, 1998 [K], 50).

These three levels of consciousness that constitute the relationship between structure and agency ultimately play a decisive role in forming "ontological security." Giddens defines the ontological security as a state in which the agent is not shrouded in insecurity, and as "a fundamental existential" environment for self and social identity (Giddens, 1998 [K], 479). Ontological security is achieved through legitimatization of actions through reflexive monitoring, or it can be achieved through routines that have been repeated for a long time in the actor's everyday living, and through the space in which such routines take place. Giddens' structuration theory has been discussed from a wide variety of angles, but what is particularly notable is the argument that because Giddens' notion of ontological security remained at the level of philosophical and abstract analyses, it is difficult to apply this theory to actual, existing social cases (Stones, 2005, 31; Urry, 1991, 71). Overcoming this requires the formation of ontology-in-suit that is implicit of the particularity of each situation (particular time/space). Universal ontological security is needed at a philosophical/theoretical level, but one might say that this calls for an expansion of the sphere of ontological perception rooted in a variety of real social situations.

Applying the theoretical framework of social structuration to the study subject of the migration and settlement of North Korean arrivals has an advantage in that it sheds light on the connection between the agency performance known as migration and settlement, on the one hand, and the particular structure of society called North Korea (or South Korea, or a third country), on the other. In particular, assuming that structure is composed of rules and resources, the study would clarify whether particular rules (symbols and norms) and resources (apparatuses of politics, economy, power, and authority) in North Korea either enabled or constrained the migration of the defecting North Koreans. (It would also clarify whether particular rules and resources in South Korea either enabled or constrained the migration.) Furthermore, such a study would provide a useful framework for analyzing how the North Korean migration changed and restructured the North Korean (or South Korean) social structure from within, especially since the late 1990s when North Koreans began defecting in large numbers. More than anything else, such a study would identify how North Korean actors in the migration-settlement experience internalize the structure and at the same time restructure it through their action, and how the actors' stocks of knowledge expand, and how they try to establish ontological security by reflexively monitoring and legitimizing their actions based on their expanded stocks of knowledge.

On the other hand, in order to capture the structure-agency relationship in the activities of the North Korean arrivals, an anthropological research methodology can be most appropriately utilized. Giddens argued that actors recognize the relationship between agency and structure, that they emphasize the reflexive monitoring in the process of legitimizing their actions, and that this process is composed of the unconscious, practical consciousness, and discursive consciousness. In particular, practical consciousness refers to the actors' recognition and monitoring of the situations and the structure around him or her (Giddens, 1998 [K]; Healey, 2006; Berger, 1995). Actors may be unable to verbally express or explain their actions, but they accept them as self-evidentially proper and right. For example, North Korean arrivals who stay in China for a period of time and engage in economic activities there unconsciously accept capitalist ideas of economy and ways of life; this in turn allows them a lead time in establishing a sense of security once they arrive in South Korea. However, because this practical consciousness is not "put into words" but only simply carried out in action, it is difficult to capture it through interviews only. For this reason, researchers try to observe the behaviors of the interviewees when they interview them and to analyze what is said in between the lines of what they say. However, it is difficult to confirm how the actor actually acts in real life. This is why ethnographic research method can be useful. By spending an appropriate amount of time together (participation-observation), and by building a personal relationship, it is possible to ascertain, through their behaviors, whether or not North Korean arrivals actually interpret and reflexively monitor the structural differences that exist between their country of origin and the country of settlement and apply the result in their agency performance.

On the other hand, the discursive consciousness refers to the actors' ability to coherently explain their actions and the reasons for them (Giddens, 1998 [K]). In other words, this refers to the organization of self-narratives of the experience of migration and settlement by the actors; an in-depth interview with a North Korean arrival provides a way of accessing the actor's discursive consciousness. LEE Yong-hwa, a staff member at Bukhan Ing-gwon Jeongbo Senteo (North Korean Human Rights Information Center), a private organization, has been conducting interviews of North Korean arrivals in South Korea. Lee states that, by the time they arrive in South Korea, most of them have gone through life-or-death experiences. He points out that North Korean arrivals instinctively know the answers that the researchers want to hear and often exaggerate their experiences accordingly, or they purposely testify inaccurately if the interviewer is not fully knowledgeable about North Korea, linguistically and otherwise (Interview with LEE Yong-hwa, 2011; YUN Taek-rim and HAHM Han-hee, 2005). To minimize dangers from such situations, it is important to recognize that what is put into words cannot be relied on to establish facts; furthermore, to verify an interviewee's narrative of experience, interviews should be conducted in multiple sessions rather than in one long session; also structured questions may expose interviewer's motives, thus interview questions should open-ended, and interviewees should be allowed to take the initiative in telling their migration experience and activities (YUN and HAHM, 2005; YANG, 2001; The Korean Council for the Women Drafted for Military Sexual Slavery by Japan 1999; YI Hee-yeong, 2011).

4. A North Korean Family in South Korea: Their Settlement Experience and Construction of Ontological Security

My study of North Korean arrivals discussed in this chapter has been conducted with the underlying framework of structuration theory described above, using ethnography. The study began in earnest in March 2011. I first surveyed the literature on the subject through archival research, and I also interviewed social workers, former and incumbent government officials, and academic researchers who have worked with North Korean arrivals for a long time. The purpose was to review the current discourses on the subject and to familiarize myself with the current state of North Korean arrivals. I then conducted participation-observation field research in a community of North Korean arrivals. The family I studied, "Family A," came to South Korea via China. The family consisted of the husband ("A," age 42), wife ("B," age 37), and son (also "A," age 12). Thus far, I have met with the family sixteen times. I met with them anywhere from a few hours at a time, to a whole day. Rapport between the researcher and the family was established based on the personal relationship that was built. The family gradually opened themselves and began speaking about their experiences and situations. The researcher did not pose structured questions but allowed conversations to take place naturally and observed their behaviors. Based on work completed so far on this study, I will now briefly examine the correlation between structure—such as capitalism, socio-cultural environment, language, and education—and the actions taken by a North Korean family in South Korea.

At the initial stage of their settlement, A's family had a relatively high level of understanding of South Korean capitalism. That is because A had long been involved in smuggling goods across the border between North Korea and China. North Korean arrivals who have experienced and known about capitalism have a much easier time settling in South Korea. Unfamiliarity with capitalist social structure is a contributing factor for the cultural maladjustment that most North Koreans in South Korea experience; most of them, in particular, have difficulty accepting the notion of economic freedom based on individual competition and responsibility, and many of them take government protection and support for granted (YI Cheol-u, 2010, 12). In the case of A, he had been going back and forth to China from North Korea. Based on his experience of trading with Chinese people and utilizing his knowledge about capitalism, he was exploring the capitalist structure of South Korean society. Thus, his desire was to find work as soon as possible. Not only that, one could see that he was collecting information on South Korean society, figuring out the kind of work he could do here and choosing where to live based on his analysis.

> *Yah* [the wife] can't work. Her health is not good. I have to start working soon. "Be-eo-ring" factory... Have you heard of it? I had an interview at Hanawon[#], and I got the job. They said the pay is 1.2 million... What kind of pay level is that? [...] At Hanawon, everybody wanted to go to Seoul, and because I was the *banjang* [class head] there I could have chosen where I wanted to go. But I told them I will not go to Seoul and that I'm coming to Bucheon. Because, small and medium-size enterprises...because of the

Hanawon is a government resettlement center for North Koreans arriving in South Korea. The first of its three locations opened in 1999 –Tr.

> small and medium-size enterprises. That is because since there are many small and medium-size enterprises [in Bucheon], I think it would be easier to find work. (Based on conversation with A, April 2011)[4]

> I tried day labor, and that's really the life of a fruit fly. Couldn't really see the end of the tunnel there. They say the government pays support when you get a license...heavy equipment... I'm going to try that. I looked into that, and as long as you have the license, they say you could easily make 3 million won per month. I'm planning on going to *hagwon* (a private institute) for that. (Based on conversation with A, August 2011)

A had a clear understanding of the importance of "money." He recited "money" as if it were a mantra, saying, for example, how one needs money to educate a child, or to settle properly. He kept trying to verify that the wage level was appropriate, and he wanted to find a more stable job and earn money. When he had money in North Korea he would spend it on buying furniture or electronic goods, but now that he is in South Korea, he said that it seems more important to keep the money on hand, and he asked this researcher about installment savings at banks and insurance products. His wife, B, also revealed a similar concern with money.

> I am looking at *Byeoruk Sijang* (Flea market, a classified advertisement newspaper -Tr.) these days. What good is it if I just stay home? It looks like it's hard for him [my husband] to do day work. Before, he told me I probably can't work. But after a few days of going to work, maybe it's really hard on him. He tells me that when my condition gets better I should find something that is not too hard. I agree with him. I feel guilty that only *ah* [the husband] works. [I'm looking] to make about 20,000 won [per day]. I was thinking about rolling *gimbab* at Gimbab Cheonguk. I'm thinking about it. (Based on conversation with B, June 2011)

---

4 At the time of this conversation, rapport had not been fully developed between the researcher and the subjects. Furthermore, upon leaving Hanawon, North Korean arrivals tend to be very suspicious of strangers. Thus, not all conversations have been recorded. The conversations quoted in this chapter represent the best reconstruction of actual conversations that took place, and the reconstructions are based partly on voice recordings and partly on my field notes. Thus, in my rendering of the conversations here, the linguistic characteristics of North Korean speech have been diluted.

> He said, let's work hard like this for three years and then open a restaurant. Like the Pyeongyang Naengmyeon place we went to with you the other time. He said we can really make lots of money then. So these days, he tells me to make this dish or that dish. He's really getting on my case. (Based on conversation with B, August 2011)

A's family shows that they recognize money as the most important factor in settling down in South Korea; they show that they also recognize and utilize, in their actions, the important principle of a capitalist society in which they must sell their labor in exchange for wages, which then allows them to support their family. Furthermore, they show that they are planning for their future. They have concluded that North Korean food is rare in South Korea and that they could utilize this rarity to open a restaurant and be financially successful. However, the labor intensity required in South Korea is a significant burden on them. A worked in a furniture store for a while. He was adamant that there was not even enough time to take a short cigarette break. He asked if all South Koreans work so hard. In the case of B, she had to stop working at a supermarket when she suddenly came down with back pain. The owner of the supermarket told her that if she cannot even handle the kind of workload there, she might as well go back to North Korea. B was insulted and felt dispirited.

North Korean arrivals' maladjustment to the unfamiliar environment of South Korea is observed in various ways. They are manifested in small incidents during the course of everyday life or through their bodily responses. For example, in the case of A's family, they suffered from severe car sickness, they could not eat South Korean food, they felt lost in large buildings, and they had headaches and other stress-related symptoms that are attributed to feelings of alienation and loneliness. In addition, in the case of B, she complained of severe physical fatigue and pain when she worked in a factory or supermarket; however, doctors did not find any serious medical problems upon examining her complaints. It seems that her physical pains in those workplaces were caused by psychological reasons, a sense of being lost, for example. Pierre Bourdieu defines "habitus" as a system of sustainable and internalized dispositions and structure, and it is embodied in the human body, and in preferences for food, clothing, and hobbies (Bourdieu, 1984; Stones, 2005). For example, when A's family moved to Bucheon after leaving Hanawon, they complained of extreme car sickness. They said that they have little experience of riding in cars, and that it was awkward for them; they also said that there was a peculiar smell in the car, and that it was making them dizzy. Thus the family showed a fear of going too far from their home, and they felt anxious about automobile transportation. In terms of food also, they hardly touched anything outside of what they made at home. Their reason is that the food in South Korea is too sweet and greasy. B laments that her son does not touch the food in school, and that he eats in great haste when he gets home from school. A sense of alienation from South Korean social and cultural environment is maximized when the family is in a building complex with bustling human traffic. In a shopping mall, or in other places where crowds gather, the couple shows bewilderment, and they say that they cannot collect their thoughts. Contrary to that, in traditional marketplaces where there are relatively fewer people shopping, or at their own home, they show a high degree of emotional security. However, stresses caused by unfamiliarity with socio-cultural environments may ease gradually as the scope of the actors' experience widens. For example, A's family carefully observe the appearance and behaviors of South Koreans around them, or those of the characters appearing in popular TV dramas; they would then use imitation as a strategy to overcome their unfamiliarity. For example, the couple tries to buy clothes for their child no matter how expensive it is, if the particular item is in fashion among the child's peer group.

Do you know what *jjoldae* pants are? That's what every child wears these

> days. We wanted him to have a pair, too, so we asked his friend's mom where we could get them. We went, and, my, they cost 150,000 won [...] You have to get *jjoldae* pants with a jacket to go with them, but they were too expensive. So we bought a pair of look-alike pants in a [traditional] market, and we just bought the jacket for 150,000 won at the store. But our neighbor, an *ajumma*, said that the *jjoldae* pants we got are a fake, and that children will ridicule our son. Is that true? I don't want our child to be made fun at... (Based on conversation with B, September 2011)

> Say, where did you get your hair cut? How much was it? ... I should cut my hair, too. I will just let it grow for now, since our circumstances are not there yet. But I want to go where you went when it's time. (Based on conversation with B, May 2011)

If the body is the canvas where *habitus* is expressed, it is evident that in the case of A's family, they are trying to gradually re-organize their own established *habitus* by imitating the appearance of South Koreans. The expansion of their experience is also slowly changing their taste in food. A's family would not touch the tempura that came with lunch boxes and would only eat plain rice. However, during the course of our repeated meetings, they were slowly adapting to South Korean food. They had resolutely stayed away from coffee before, but now it has become a requisite drink after meals, as is the case for many South Koreans. The car sickness they suffered disappeared completely six months after leaving Hanawon.

On the other hand, if language operates as a structure that either constraints or enables action, in the case of A's family, their agency performance is constrained by the language used in South Korea. Among themselves, the family uses a language that was distinct from what was used in South Korea. They express frustration at not being able to understand what people said in South Korea. They have a difficult time understanding the language when they went shopping or when they met with South Korean people, and their son demanded that the couple, who speak with strong North Korean accents, learn "South Korean."

> For the life of me, I can't understand what they say. They use so many foreign words... I have to learn that thing, English. If I can't, at least our son has to speak English. (Based on conversation with B, May 2011)

> (On the way back from clothes shopping for their son at E-Mart) We couldn't have bought this if it weren't for you [the researcher]. Couldn't tell what they were saying. So complicated, and can't understand their explanation... (Based on conversation with A, May 2011)

However, active agency performance on the part of the actors in regards to the language structure was also observed. For example, the family would imitate "South Korean style of speaking," or they would speak in low voices in public spaces so as to not reveal their North Korean accents. Also, the son was quickly getting used to South Korean-style language, and A and B were trying to imitate South Korean accents as their child was teaching them. Despite their efforts, while words in South Korean style of language can be gradually learned, one's manner of speaking and accents cannot be easily corrected. Thus, in job interviews, or when they met with strangers, the couple sometimes introduced themselves as ethnic Koreans from China. They recognized the problem with the language as revealed in the following conversation with this researcher:

> This morning, his friends came over and he said, "Mom speaks with at least some semblance to South Korean speech, but Dad's South Korean is really awkward." Then he told his father not to speak. Can you believe that?!... (Based on conversation with A, May 2011)

After constantly monitoring their language and checking responses from people around them A's family decided to speak in low voices in restaurants or other such public places where crowds gather. When they first left Hanawon, the couple often spoke about "When I was in North Korea...," specifically point- ing out North Korea in their speech. However, in the process of their settlement, they gradually replaced "North Korea" with demonstrative nouns such as "there," or "that place." It seems that they gradually came to recognize what North Korean language and accents mean in South Korea.

Lastly, educational issues in South Korea are becoming structural constraints for A's family. A and his wife B came to South Korea out of their utter devotion and love for their son. They said that as economic conditions in North Korea deteriorated, the social environment became panic-stricken; they said that if the condition continued they feared that it would have bad effect on their son, and that is why they decided to come to South Korea. However, the competition in education was far more overheated than they had thought, and they were frustrated that they have no way of knowing if their child was doing well or not at school.

> I came here because of [our son]. It seems to me that he would live a life that is similar to mine if we stayed in North Korea. I want our [son] to study hard, make lots of money, and become a leader... But I don't know anything, and I don't know what I should be doing for him... (Based on conversation with B, June 2011)

However, the educational system in South Korea and the family's lack of information and experience in the South Korean education system is a source of endless insecurity for them. They heard that their son's friends go to *hagwon*, but they did not know what kind of place it is and worried about whether or not their son would be able to keep up if they sent him there. At around this time, they came up with a solution, which was to have private tutors for their son. The couple asked the researcher to find a private tutor; they wanted to find a place where their son could receive private lessons free of charge.

> He should be educated, even if that means we have to have private tutors for English and Math. He's always been into playing, and playing only. When we were in North Korea, we had private tutors for him, and the tutor taught him as if our son was his/her own. But in South Korea, even that is not possible. I'm afraid we'll ruin him at this rate. (Based on conversation with

A, June 2011)

They constantly checked if their son was doing well in and out of the classroom at school, and they proactively sought ways to help him. They made frequent visits to see their son's homeroom teacher, again indicating that they actively sought solutions to deal with educational issues in particular. In October of 2011, A (the son) had brought home a good score on a math test, and B was very happy and said that all her insecurities and worries disappeared upon receiving the good news. Her position was that it does not matter how hard it is for them to adjust to South Korea, as long as A (the son) is doing well in school, she feels that their hardship is compensated. Of course, the fact that A is doing well in school is meaningful in that it is also an indication that he is doing well in adapting to South Korea. However, it is noteworthy that the parents measure justification for their migration based on the level of the child's adaptation to the new place.

Lack of information on South Korean social structure—as examined above in terms of capitalism, sociocultural environment, language, and education—is a significant constraint on their agency performance. A traveled to China frequently on trading trips, and B's family moved to China a long time ago; in other words, they were quite knowledgeable about Chinese-style capitalism. Despite this background, it seems that it is not easy for this couple to internalize South Korean social structure in a short time. Furthermore, Chinese-style capitalism, mixed with socialism, has been introduced to a significant degree to North Korea, and they were able to adapt to it without much difficulty. However, in South Korea, the extremely competitive neo-liberal capitalist system puts them in a condition of extreme confusion all the time. In addition, the North Korea-China border area is a place where the two cultures mix quite well together, and the socio-cultural environment there was not so alien to the couple. Also, the language of the ethnic Koreans living in the three northeast provinces of China is a language North Koreans are familiar with, and it gave them a significant sense of security. On the contrary, they have experienced significant differences in South Korean social structure from what they have experienced in North Korea or in another country they stayed in the route to South Korea. This has been a cause of frequent arguments lately between the husband and wife, who have had a relatively good relationship in the past. The cause of their arguments is often derived from the difference in how they each recognize South Korean society. For example, the wife is wary of anyone who approaches them and volunteers to help them. She says she cannot trust South Koreans because there is no such thing as free lunch for South Koreans. On the other hand, the husband, who traded for a long time in North Korea and China, is of the opinion that if someone is sincere in trying to help them, they have to trust that person and work together. The husband and wife routinely argue because of this difference.

The lack of information and experience on the society they are newly trying to adapt to not only constrains their agency performance, but it is also the decisive factor that heightens their sense of insecurity. Their attempts to overcome their insecurity —such as finding a job to engage in economic activities, imitating the appearance of South Koreans and other efforts to get used to the unfamiliar environment, attempts to speak like South Koreans, seeking outside help for their child's education—go through stages of trial and error and are performed in repetition, and eventually they become a new routine for them. It has been approximately eight months since A's family left Hanawon, and they are finding their own ways of instituting routine. Although he moved his job many times, A has been working continuously; B's insecurity, which had been accompanied by physical symptoms, has been noticeably relieved. In the case of the child, he had been taunted by a few older students, which gave him some grief, but he is gradually adapting to school life in South Korea. Recently, with the subsidy they received from the government and a month's wages that A earned from working in a furniture store, the family bought a complete set of furniture including beds, sofa, desk, and wardrobe. B was happy and said that now she has furniture, she feels that this is her home. She said that before there was the feeling of constantly wandering around, and now she feels that her life (space of routine) is here. Their daily activities and the space of activities thus formed gradually contributed to re-organizing their ontological security, and by going through this process the family is slowly settling down in South Korea. It goes without saying that stability for their family is still far off, and the family has yet to overcome many hurdles before their life in South Korea becomes stable. However, it is clear that they are not simply passive agents who adapt to South Korean structure, and that their agency re-constructs/re-produces South Korean social structure in various ways (Giddens, 1976; Stones 2007, 20). Given that this is the case, their agency will usher much change in South Korean society. In this context—that is, seen within the framework of a dialectical relationship of agency and structure—it would certainly be possible to break away from a Cold War perspective and re-construct social structure to understand the North Korean arrivals from a multicultural perspective. The topic of how such possibility is realized—or how North Korean arrivals' repeated agent actions are structured in reality, and what structures they reproduce—is outside of the scope of this chapter, and it remains a topic for future examination in follow-up studies.

5. Conclusion

There are now approximately 20,000 North Korean arrivals living in South Korea. The need for in-depth sociological studies on the phenomenon of their migration and settlement cannot be overemphasized. The migration-settlement experience of the North

Korean arrivals has much to suggest, that no other migration group can offer. What makes their experience unique is that it is very much a part of the Cold War North-South Korea confrontation that is being played out in the post-Cold War era. Furthermore, their experience is also being played out on the terrains of Cold War-era Northeast Asia politics in the post-Cold War period. The grand narratives of post-Cold War, Cold War, and Northeast Asia politics are translated in everyday life as food, language, life style, education, and family. Agents accept, resist, or negotiate with these structures in everyday moments in their own ways. In other words, the everyday world of their migration-settlement experience is a space where one can see ruptures in post-Cold War and Cold War narratives, and it is also a sphere of constant relationship between agent and social structure.

In migration studies thus far, there have been various attempts to study the somewhat unique migration motives and trajectories, and the settlement experiences and processes, of North Koreans who defect from their country. However, in the cases of studies that relied on migration study models that are widely used in the West, they often fail to capture the particular migration-settlement experience of the North Koreans; on the other hand, the studies that attempted to overcome this limitation by focusing on case studies or on identifying "the state of affairs" fail to capture the North Korean migration experience at the level of their everyday living. This chapter argues that Western paradigms of migration study should be adapted to fit the particular local context, and this study has shown, using the framework of the social structuration theory and through a case study of a North Korean family living in South Korea, how migration-settlement agency and social structure are structuralized through mutual interaction, and how they reconstruct their routine and build ontological security through this. This study confirms that social structures do not simply either constrain or enable agency, but they interact with agency to be utilized as resources in the next stage of agent actions; this shows that the social structuration approach is a sociological framework that could explain, at the everyday level, the settlement process of North Koreans arrivals who have to adapt to a new environment in South Korea.

Also, there is a need to emphasize once again the importance of utilizing ethnography, given that North Korean arrivals do not easily reveal their experiences due to the dangers they experienced during the course of their migration and settlement process; one has to also take into consideration that migration-settlement is a phenomena that is identified and experienced in everyday living. It goes without saying that studying the migration and settlement phenomenon of North Koreans who defect from their country through ethnography and in-depth interviews is no simple matter. Even if one puts aside the issue of difficulty accessing the subject population, there are other obstacles and possible pitfalls that one must be mindful of such as misunderstandings caused by language difference; the North Koreans arrivals' guarded attitudes toward strangers; and the possibility that the interviewees may be giving distorted answers, partly due to the fact that they may have participated in countless number of interviews and opinion surveys. The difficulties such a study poses are various and hard to predict. Furthermore, ethnographic methods (in particular participation-observation) and in-depth interviews have not been used widely in sociology because the academic field of sociology, which has long been dominated by empiricist studies, has been viewed as lacking objectivity; the "instant narratives" and answers given in an interview situation can change depending on the interview situation and who is being interviewed, and for a long time the approach has been criticized as unscientific. Despite these criticisms, the in-depth interview method is now widely utilized in studies that try to understand the lives of social minorities because it allows the researcher to capture actual social mechanisms and personal experience of the subject's life within the context of the interviewee's own system of meaning. What one has to be careful about is that the experience explained by the interviewee in such an interview is not necessarily factual but an interpretation; also, when an interviewee is referring to an experience in the past, one has to remember that the interviewee is "introducing by (re-) interpreting" in a "particular manner" a "particular content" among a long list of contents they must have experienced throughout his or her long life cycle, from the perspective of the "present" (YI Hee-yeong, 2011, 220). Also, to make sure that the study does not become a list of speculative stories or minor issues, it is important to have in place a solid theoretical/analytical framework that is rooted in complexities of social structure (YI Hee-yeong, 2011; Peukert, 2003 [K]). In this chapter, I have tried to capture, using ethnographic methodologies, the migration and settlement experiences of North Korean arrivals within the framework of the dialectical relationship between agency and structure. I believe such an attempt is meaningful in that while it takes into consideration the historical and social context of the region where defecting North Koreans gain signification as a migration group, it examines at the same time the everyday experiences of the North Korean arrivals from the perspective of their relationship to social structure.

Bibliography

1. Korean

AHN Jong-su (2010), "Bukhan sijanghwa wa jumin saenghwal eseo ui byeonhwa" (Marketization of North Korea and changes in the people's lives in North Korean), *Bukhan jumin ui saenghwal byeonhwa wa nambuk sotong ui gil* (Changes in North Korean people's living and path of North-South Korean communication), Proceedings of the 2010 Academic Conference on Commemorating Manhae.

EOM Tae-wan (2010), *Talbuk nanmin ui wigijeok gyeongheom gwa wisang* (North Korean refugees' experience of crises and their status), Seoul: Gyeongnam Daehakkyo Chulpanbu (Kyungnam University Press).

GIDDENS, Anthony Giddens (Aenssoni GIDEUNS) (1998), *Sahoe guseongron* (Social structuration theory), Seoul: Jeojak Academie. [This work is cited as Giddens (1998) [K] in the text to denote that a Korean translation was used –Tr.]

GWAK Hae-ryong (2005), *Bukhan ital jumin hyeonhwang gwa munje: sarye wa jiwon bangan* (The current state and issues of North Korean arrivals: Case studies and support measures), Seoul: Korean Studies Information.

IM Chae-wan and CHOE Yeong-gwan (2000), "Jungguk nae takbukja ui 'nanminjeok' sanghwang gwa geu daechek: Yeonbeon jachiju jiyeok josar eul jungsim euro" (The "refugee" situation of North Korean arrivals in China and solutions for the situation: A study based on survey of the Yanbian Autonomous Region), *Tongil munje yeongu* (The Korean Journal of Unification Affairs), *36*, 121-151.

JEON U-taek *et al.* (2010), *Tongil silheom: geu chil nyeon* (The seven years of unification experimentation), Seoul: Hanul.

JEONG Ju-sin (2009), *Talbukja munje ui insik 1&2* (Understanding the issues of North Koreans defecting from North Korea 1 & 2), Seoul: Prima.

____________ (2005), "Bukhan ital jumin ui namhan sahoe jeongchak eul wihan sahoeh wa gwajeong il gochal" (A study on socialization process by North Korean arrivals for settlement in South Korean society), *Tongil jeonryak* (Unification Strategy), *5*(2), 229-257.

JO Jeong-a et al., *Bukhan jumin ui uisik gwa jeongcheseong: ja-a-ui dognip, gukga ui geuneul, yongmang ui busang* (North Korean citizen consciousness and identity: Self independence, the shadow of the state, and the rise of desire), Seoul: Korea Institute for National Unification.

Joeun beot deul (Good Friends) (1999), Duman gang eul geon-eoon saram deul: Jungguk dongbukbu jiyeok 2,479-gae maeul bukhan "singnyang nanmin" siltae josa (People who have come across the Duman River: A fact-finding survey of North Korean "food refugees" in 2,479 villages in northeastern region of China), Seoul: Jeongto Chulpan (Jeongto Press).

KIM In-sung (2005), "Talbukja hyeonhwang bunseok: talbuk, junggan gichak, jeongchak ggajiui jeon gwajeongui chongchejeok bunseok" (Analysis of the current state of North Korean arrivals: comprehensive analysis of the entire process of defecting from North Korea, making temporary stopovers, and settlement), In *Minjok Yeonku* (The Study of the Nation), *14*, 6-34.

KIM Yun-yeong (2002), "Talbuk adong deul ui namhan hakgyo saenghwal gwa jeongcheseong" (North Korean children's school life in South Korea and their identity) (Master's thesis), Graduate School of Cultural Anthropology, Hanyang University.

Korea Cheongshindae's Institute and The Korean Council for the Women Drafted for Military Sexual Slavery by Japan (Han'guk jeongsindae yeonguso and Han'guk jeongsindae munje daechek hyeobuihoe) (1999), Gangjero kkeul-ryeogan Joseonin gun wianbu deul 3 (The people of Joseon who were forcibly taken as military comfort women 3), Seoul: Hanul.

NOH Gwi-nam (2011), "Yeoseong ui gonggan gyeongheom hwakjang gwa uisik byeonhwa" (The expansion of women's spatial experience and consciousness change).

PARK Yun-suk and YUN In-jin (2007), "Takbuk cheongsonyeon ui sahoe jeok jiji teukseong gwa namhan sahoe jeogeung gwa ui gwang'ye" (Correlation between characteristics of social support for North Korean youths in South Korea and their social adaptation), *Han'guk Sahoehak* (Korean Journal of Sociology), *41*(1), 124-155.

Peukert, D. (Poikereuteu) (2003), *Nachi sidae ui ilsangsa: sun-eung, jeohang, injongjuui* (Everyday life during the Nazi era: Conformation, resistance, and racism), KIM Hagi (Trans.), Seoul: Gaemagowon. [This work is cited as Peukert (2003) [K] in the text to denote that a Korean translation was used −Tr.]

YANG Hyeon-a (2001), "Jeungeon gwa yeoksa sseuigi: Han'gugin 'gun wianbu' ui jucheseong jaehyeon" (Testimony and history writing: Reconstructing the identity of Korean "army comfort women"), *Sahoewa Yeoksa* (Society and History), *60*, 60-96.

YI Cheol-u (2010), "Bukhan jumin e daehan ihae" (Understanding North Koreans), Han'guk sahoe bokjisa hyeophoe (The Association of Korean Social Workers), *Bukhan ital jumin seobiseu jeonmun illyeok yangseong gicho gyoyuk* (Primary education for cultivating specialists serving North Korean arrivals), Seoul: Han'guk sahoe bokjisa hyeophoe (The Association of Korean Social Workers).

YI Cheol-u (2011), "Bukhan jumin e daehan ihae" (Understanding North Koreans), Han'guk sahoe bokjisa hyeophoe (The Association of Korean Social Workers), *Bukhan ital jumin seobiseu jeonmun illyeok yangseong gicho gyo-*

yuk (Primary education for cultivating specialists serving North Korean arrivals), Seoul: Han'guk sahoe bokjisa hyeophoe (The Association of Korean Social Workers).

YI Geum-sun and YUN Yeo-sang (2006), "Bukhan jumin ui gukgyeong idong gwa cheobeol siltae" (Border-crossing by North Koreans and how they are punished), *Tongil munje yeongu* (The Korean Journal of Unification Affairs), *18*(1), 217-252.

YI Hee-yeong (2011), "Bukhan ilsang saenghwal yeon'gu jaryo saengseong gwa haeseok: gusul jaryo yeon'gu bangbeobnon eul jungsim euro" (Generation and interpretation of research data on North Korean everyday life: With focus on the methodology of studying oral data) in PARK Sunseong and HONG Min, *Oechim gwa soksagim: Bukhan ui ilsang saenghwal segye* (Shouts and whispers: The everyday world of North Korea), Seoul: Hanul.

YI Yong-ho (2002), "Nanmin ui gaenyeom gwa boho" (The concept and protection of refugees), Gukje beobhakhoe ronbo (The Journal of the The Korean Society of International Law), *52*(2), 311-338.

YUN In-jin (2009), *Bukhan ijumin* (North Korean migrants), Seoul: Jimmundang.

YUN Tak-rim and HAHM Han-hee (2005), "Nambukhan yeoseong saenghwal munhwa ui ihae: jiban il gwa yuga reul jungsim euro" (Understanding everyday cultures of women in South and North Korea: With focus on household chores and child-rearing), *Gajok gwa munhwa* (Family and Culture), *17*(2), 3-32.

2. English

Berger, R. (1995), "Agency, structure, and Jewish survival of the Holocaust: a life history study," *The Sociological Quarterly*, *36*(1), 15-36.

Bourdieu, P. (1977), *Outline of a theory of practice*. Cambridge: Cambridge University Press.

________ (1984), *Distinction: a social critique of the judgment of taste*, London: Routledge.

Healey, R. (2006), "Asylum-seekers and refugees: a structuration theory analysis of their experiences in the UK," *Population, Space and Place, 12*, 257-271.

Ritzer, G. (2000), *Modern sociological theory* (5th ed), New York: McGraw-Hill Higher Education.

Stones, R. (2005), *Structuration theory*, Basingstoke: Palgrave.

Urry, J. (1991), "Time and space in Giddens' social theory," In C.G.A. Bryant and D. Jary (Eds), *Giddens' theory of structuration: a critical appreciation*, London: Routledge.